Praise for
Ultimate Classroom Control Handbook

"I can honestly say that once I started this book, I could not put it down. The techniques for handling disruptive classroom behavior are outstanding and very workable, not only in a educational/school setting but also in many other areas of life where groups of teenagers are together...The techniques show that kind words, respect, and consistency go a long way in handling out-of-control teenagers...Many of the ideas will work just as well on special education students as the average teen."

—Sherry Odom, Huntsville Independent School District,
Special Education Department

"Practical ideas to use everyday in the classroom to help all students be successful. Dave Foley not only explains how to use his strategies, he gives actual examples of what to do and say within the classroom environment."

—Kathleen Clark, Teacher, Department of Family & Consumer Sciences,
Charleston High School

"Very reader-friendly...The format makes it easy to go back to a particular topic and review it quickly. The inclusion of information on both junior high and high school student behaviors and attitudes is especially welcome...Very useful for even veteran teachers because...it is good to add some new things to our bag of tricks."

—Valerie Vuicich, Director of Operations, State Center Consortium

"A must-read for new middle school and junior high teachers...Filled with every possible scenario a teacher could come across...Quick, easy solutions that keep your classroom running smoothly and keep your students learning."

—Renee Gussert, Elementary/Middle School Teacher, Cadillac Schools

ULTIMATE
Classroom
Control
HANDBOOK

A Veteran Teacher's On-the-Spot Techniques for Solving Adolescent Student Misbehavior

Foreword by Laura Stewart, Masters of Education, Certificate of Advanced Study from Harvard University

DAVE FOLEY

JIST Works

America's Career Publisher

Ultimate Classroom Control Handbook

A Veteran Teacher's On-the-Spot Techniques for Solving Adolescent Student Misbehavior

© 2007 by Dave Foley

Published by JIST Works, an imprint of JIST Publishing, Inc.
8902 Otis Avenue
Indianapolis, IN 46216-1033
Phone: 1-800-648-JIST   Fax: 1-800-JIST-FAX   E-mail: info@jist.com

Visit our Web site at **www.jist.com** for information on JIST, free job search tips, book excerpts, and how to order our many products! For free information on 14,000 job titles, visit **www.careeroink.com.**

Quantity discounts are available for JIST books. Have future editions of JIST books automatically delivered to you on publication through our convenient standing order program. Please call our Sales Department at 1-800-648-5478 for a free catalog and more information.

Note to Teachers, Principals, School Administrators, and College Educators

- Get free guidance on running an in-service meeting on classroom management at your school using the proven techniques in *Ultimate Classroom Control Handbook*. Available at www.jist.com.

- Get a free instructor's guide and lesson plans for using *Ultimate Classroom Control Handbook* in a teacher education course on classroom management or as part of a general teacher education curriculum. Available at www.jist.com.

Acquisitions Editor: Susan Pines   Development Editor: Heather Stith
Interior Designer: designLab   Page Layout: Trudy Coler
Proofreader: Paula Lowell   Indexer: Cheryl Lenser
Printed in the United States of America

12 11 10 09 08 07 06   9 8 7 6 5 4 3 2 1

Library of Congress Cataloging-in-Publication Data

Foley, Dave, 1947-

   Ultimate classroom control handbook : a veteran teacher's on-the-spot techniques for solving adolescent student misbehavior / Dave Foley.

      p. cm.

   Includes index.

   ISBN-13: 978-1-59357-338-6 (alk. paper)

   ISBN-10: 1-59357-338-3 (alk. paper)

   1. Classroom management--United States--Handbooks, manuals, etc. 2. School discipline--United States--Handbooks, manuals, etc. I. Title.

   LB3013.F64 2006

   373.1102'4--dc22

                              2006015545

ISBN-13: 978-1-59357-338-6; ISBN-10: 1-59357-338-3

Solve the Most Unpredictable Classroom Management Problems Instantly, So You Can Get Back to Teaching

Ultimate Classroom Control Handbook was not hypothesized in a college classroom or developed by a committee of educational theorists. Rather its techniques and ideas came from spending 29 years as a classroom teacher working with middle school and junior high school students. In addition, for most of those years, I was coaching cross-country and track teams at the junior and senior high school level. Prior to and during my first years of teaching, I spent nine summers as a camp counselor living in cabin groups with boys ranging from 11 to 17 at an outdoor YMCA camp. These varied experiences taught me much about why adolescents do what they do and how they can be motivated to respond to leadership.

In my attempt to get my students to behave, come to class ready to work, and turn their assignments in on time, I tried all sorts of techniques, applied various educational philosophies, and basically experimented until things began to improve. I borrowed ideas from others, improvised, and sometimes just relied on my instincts.

As I began to put together this troubleshooting guide for teachers, I focused on what I was doing with classroom management on a day-to-day basis and asked my colleagues for their ideas. Sometimes we would trade our favorite techniques for working with students the way most people trade recipes. I discovered that the best teachers are true pragmatists. Instead of trying to teach according to any particular theory, they are guided by the principle of "If it works and helps me be a more effective teacher, I'll try it."

What you will find in this helpful, sometimes humorous fix-it handbook are techniques that have been successful for teachers in the trenches working to educate adolescent students.

Dedication

To my wife and best friend, Cyndy.

Acknowledgements

This manuscript wouldn't exist were it not for an excellent student teacher of mine, Mindy Cucinnella, who gave me the impetus to start writing down my thoughts on classroom management. It wouldn't have ever been a published book had not my sister-in-law Sallie Foley, a successful author herself, convinced me that I had something a publisher could use and then provided encouragement as I soldiered through the writing of the book proposal.

I am deeply grateful to the staff of JIST Publishing, notably acquisitions editor, Susan Pines, for all her encouragement and help; developmental editor, Heather Stith, for offering her editing expertise; and Dave Anderson, for helping me prepare some extras to make the book more user-friendly.

My special thanks goes to Laura Stewart, Leta Corwin, Bruce Loper, and Penny Phelps. These teachers in the Cadillac Schools made sure that only ideas that were relevant to successful teaching were included in the manuscript. I am also indebted to all those kids who populated my classes and were a part of teams I coached during my 29 years in education. Without them, I would have had nothing to write about.

I am also deeply grateful to my parents, Bunny and Norm Foley, who taught me that love was the key ingredient in effective parenting. Finally, thanks to my children, Ben and Betsy, and my wife, Cyndy, for bringing so much joy to my life.

CONTENTS

Foreword

Mr. Foley is a good liar. I worked with him for 15 years, and there was no end to the lies he told students. Some gullible eighth graders were always looking for the secret passageway to the alleged old bowling alley under the cafeteria. They eventually learned not to believe everything they were told.

You, however, can believe the wise, practical advice in this book. Read it, and you will find gems of knowledge pertaining to early teen behavior and classroom management. Use what fits your style. Discipline is an art, and I have always believed the best way to learn student discipline is to ask veteran teachers.

Mr. Foley didn't just teach; he set an example. In our small town, he is a legend in his own time. Every day he would either run or canoe the 12 miles round trip to our school on the lake. He was teacher of the year and has been admitted to the school's Coaching Hall of Fame. He won the town's triathlon last summer, beating men almost a third his age. And did I mention he is a snowshoe racer? (Yes, that means running miles up and down hills on snowshoes!)

When he went up on stage to receive his teacher of the year award, his cross-country team, as a surprise to him, stood behind him in their best suits. They knew him as a teacher who truly cared. He had disciplined them both on and off the field with respect, and they respected him for it. Now he has written this book to share his experience with you.

Laura Stewart, Masters of Education,
Certificate of Advanced Study from Harvard University

Introduction

Few teachers enjoy being disciplinarians. They would rather teach than spend time and energy levying punishment. After all, their job description clearly identifies their work as teaching, not disciplining. The goal of this book is to equip teachers with classroom management strategies so they can devote more hours to instructing and waste less time dealing with student misbehavior. Teachers learn how to deal with behavior issues so that discipline consequences are prompt and immediate. In this way the problems end, and the lesson continues. In most cases, there is no paperwork involved in these solutions and no conference with parents, administrators, or students. The behavior problem is settled in the classroom, and time outside of class isn't tied up resolving discipline issues with students.

At the present time teachers and school districts need all the help they can get as federal programs such as the No Child Left Behind Act and various state and local government mandates put schools under increased pressure to produce high test scores. Curriculum, teaching methods, and even the teachers themselves receive more scrutiny. If student achievement drops or fails to improve fast enough, school districts may lose funding, get restructured, or, in a worst-case scenario, be dissolved.

Yet the best lesson plans in the world won't succeed if student misbehavior hamstrings an educator's attempts to teach. Good classroom management practices are vital to creating an environment where students can learn. The ideas and techniques in this book may not guarantee that your students' test scores will rise to the top percentile, but they do offer strategies that will enable you to conduct class in an atmosphere where students can attend to their schoolwork without disruption.

The Nature of Adolescents

The only thing predictable about adolescents is their unpredictability. Adolescence is a time of tremendous change. In almost every class of students, there will be individuals who are model citizens and those whose development you would swear stopped somewhere around the age of eight. Because the model citizens won't impede your teaching, you will find yourself focusing on those students whose natural impulses are not to sit back and absorb the lessons you're teaching.

High Energy

Although some adolescents are lethargic and sit there with that no-one-home look, most are energized beings. Much of what constitutes misbehavior occurs because the bulk of a student's school experience consists of sitting quietly for nearly an hour and then getting a short break before spending another hour in a seat. Kids under the age of 16 are, by nature, active individuals who want to talk, move around, and choose their activities. Six or seven class periods of sit-down time every day works totally against their nature.

As a group, young adolescents also distract easily and possess short attention spans. This becomes apparent when you give directions for an assignment. Once is never enough. Immediately after saying the instructions, expect to hear a chorus of "Can you say that again? What page is it?" or "Do we have any homework?" queries.

As the teacher, you are faced with having to harness this energy in the classroom without stifling your students' enthusiasm. Fortunately, most adolescents still want to please adults and love to be praised. In my eighth grade class discussions, when I asked a question, those who thought their answer was anywhere near correct immediately waved a hand in the air. If I needed to have someone pass out textbooks or run an errand to the office, I would have a flock of volunteers. Give kids some recognition, a compliment about their schoolwork, or a positive comment on their performance in a music or sports competition, and they will be genuinely pleased.

Focus on Peers

Adolescents make a concerted effort to be less dependent on their parents. Increasingly, these youth turn away from adults as they seek to build close relationships with their peers. When you're in a classroom outnumbered 30-to-1, being an adult can be pretty lonely while adolescents are going through this process of pulling away from adults and bonding with peers.

Even though they want to be more independent, students are less willing to accept responsibility for their mistakes. If a student receives a low test grade or a discipline write-up, he will blame your teaching, his parents, the other students, or anybody else but him for his predicament. The attitude seems to be, "How can you do this to me?"

Much of what students do in your classroom is a performance to impress their fellow students. Adolescent social climbing goes on every minute of every day as students seek to reach a better social station, become part of the "in" crowd, and gain peer approval. Sometimes these performances involve the teacher, as a student will try to make a teacher feel flustered, embarrassed, or angry. Another target is their classmates. Not everyone can be in the "in" crowd, or it would lose its exclusiveness, so individuals and sometimes groups of students are put down, criticized, or ridiculed.

To gain peer acceptance, some students act out in an effort to establish some sort of identity or notoriety. Adolescents are desperate to win approval, respect, or just recognition. The artist, the musician, the athlete, the brain, and the fashionista are common roles that generally don't pose problems. Those who seek to be known as the class clown, the troublemaker, or the tough kid provide a real challenge to teachers.

The Opposite Sex

The middle school/junior high years also bring the first signs of a sexual awakening among the student population. The girls get interested first. However, the boys, who tend to be a year or so behind in their overall emotional development already, remain, for the most part, blissfully unaware of the girls' new interest. It is an exasperating time for these maturing girls as they realize that the boys their age are way too childish.

Typically most of the dating interest in these girls comes from older high school boys. It's not that the younger boys aren't interested; it's just that they haven't figured out how to interact appropriately with girls. Especially among seventh and eighth graders, the boys will grab the girls' pencils or notebooks, playfully jab at them, or maybe try to trip them. This primitive display of interest just makes the girls mad and puzzles the boys. When your students are in the midst of this early stage of hormonal action, whatever you're teaching seems irrelevant to them.

The Effect of Teachers

Students often exhibit Jekyll and Hyde tendencies. They can be model citizens in one classroom and then suddenly become like wild things in the next class. The teacher's mastery of classroom management, or the lack of it, provides the key to the puzzle. Although those who teach by intimidation, the ones whom students call mean teachers, get the job done, theirs is not a role that most teachers, including myself, want to adopt.

Teachers whom students like and respect tend to have fewer discipline problems. Not all students strive to be teacher pleasers, but most students find it harder to deliberately disrupt the class of popular staff members. In addition, liking a teacher may motivate students to put forth more effort in their studies.

Over the next 18 chapters you will find a comprehensive action plan for classroom management that I developed through trial and error over the 29 years I spent as a middle school and junior high school teacher. Keep in mind that classroom management never ends. It is not a system that once implemented doesn't need to be revisited. Even though it is an ongoing task, gradually it will get easier as your students discover that misbehavior leads to consequences they would rather avoid. The purpose of this plan is to enable you to spend more time teaching and less time dealing with student problems.

PART I

Helping Students to Behave

I n a perfect world, people would do things just because they should. However, like most adults, my motivation for paying taxes, buying a fishing license, and not leaving my car in a "no parking" zone is to avoid unpleasant legal consequences.

Students function similarly in that they will behave well in order to avoid having unpleasant things happen to them. In a classroom setting, these unpleasant things include having to stay after class, having to move away from friends, and having their classmates disapprove of them.

The fear of being sent to the office or having the teacher call a parent to discuss behavior problems can also bring about improvement in classroom behavior. Misbehavior also disappears when teachers offer incentives. Although situations sometimes dictate that misbehaving students be sent to the office or have their parents called, the solid classroom management program presented in the first eight chapters of this book allows teachers to deal effectively with most disruptions without taking the matter beyond the classroom walls.

Managing Student Behavior

Do you find that all your students want to do is fool around while you're trying to teach? Does it take forever to get your students to settle down? If you answered yes to either of these questions, you're not alone. Teachers have been voicing these complaints since the days of the one-room schoolhouse. These problems are not about to go away, because, with the possible exception of a few highly motivated high school juniors and seniors, kids do not naturally settle down and pay attention in class. Yet somehow we teachers are expected to keep these kids focused on our lessons. Good, creative lesson plans help, but even master teachers have to use certain techniques to keep their classes attentive. This chapter lays the groundwork for the basic strategies you can use to control your classroom.

The Truth About Classroom Rules

When I first began teaching, I would post a list of class rules and give a copy of that list to each student. On the first day of classes, I would stand at the front of the classroom and recite the litany, telling students that they should be in their seat when the bell rings and should not eat, drink, throw stuff, play with the heater blower, lean back on their chairs, or talk when a lesson was being taught or another student was reciting. Then I gave them the exception rules, which covered the things they could do at certain times. For instance, students couldn't leave their seats to throw stuff in the wastebasket or sharpen their pencils when I was talking. However, they could do these things at other times. The class rules list looked easy enough to understand when I was creating it; however, as soon I began to explain the rules, the hands started waving.

"Mr. Foley, if we can't sharpen our pencil when you're talking, can we sharpen it when you're answering a question?"

"Mr. Foley, is sucking on a cough drop considered eating?"

"Mr. Foley, is it talking if I tell someone that he's on the wrong page while you're talking?"

"Is whispering talking? Even if the only one who can hear me is the one I'm whispering to?"

They studied my rules like lawyers looking for loopholes. For example, if the rule stated that students couldn't leave their seats while I was talking, invariably some student would start sliding his desk around the room while still seated. When I would call him on that, he would say, "But the rule says you can't leave your seat. I'm still in my seat."

At first, I responded to the students' actions by adding to the list of rules. But the more I tried to have a rule for every infraction, the more exceptions I found. The list of rules kept growing until I had more than 20 of them. The rules became so confusing that sometimes I wasn't even sure what I meant. I finally just took a look at my rules and asked myself, "Just what are you trying to do?" The answer that came to me was very simple. All I wanted to do was to be able to teach in an environment where neither my students nor I would be distracted.

The next year I came to school with just one rule: *"If you make it so I can't teach effectively or you or other students can't learn effectively, then there is a problem."* (Several years later I heard the noted educator Jim Fay speak on "Love and Logic" at a conference and discovered that I had unknowingly adopted one of his core principles. As I became familiar with Fay's Love and Logic method, I discovered more similarities in our approaches to classroom management.) I would defend this all-encompassing rule by saying something like, *"It doesn't take much to distract my classes because I'm so boring."* I would then hand a kid a paper wad and have him shoot it toward the wastebasket. Everybody watched. Then I would have a student walk from his seat to the pencil sharpener, sharpen a pencil, and return to his seat. Again all eyes were on the student. *"If you noticed,"* I would continue, *"you can't help but watch a paper wad arcing toward the basket or a classmate walking across the room, because those things are vastly more interesting than hearing me talk or another student recite. So you can see, if you're ever going to learn anything in this class, you're going to have to just sit there when I'm teaching. I'll try to be funny and interesting, but you can see that I have a long way to go."*

Consistency

No matter how consistent you try to be with your discipline, you are not going to catch every kid who misbehaves. In my talks about discipline with my students, I never promised to deal with every instance of class misbehavior. Rather, I told them my role was similar to the highway patrolman, and my students were like drivers on the road. The patrolman can ticket anyone who drives over the speed limit, but not all speeders are ticketed. The student who disrupts class may not be caught and punished, just as someone who disregards traffic signals or speed limits may not be ticketed. But just like drivers who choose to drive too fast, students who misbehave in class will have to suffer the consequences if they're caught.

The reason I told my students about the highway patrolman is that I knew there would be times when I would be so involved in my teaching that I either might not see misbehavior or might choose to ignore it. I occasionally ignored minor misbehavior because I realized that if I stopped to address the behavior problem, I might lose the momentum of the lesson I was presenting or might simply forget the point I was trying to make. If I were to tell my class that everyone who talks stays after class, then invariably when I disciplined Jacob, he would point out that I didn't discipline Travis whom I ignored when he was misbehaving earlier. The students needed to know that, like the highway patrolman, I might not address every infraction.

Follow-Through

Classroom misbehavior needs to be addressed on a regular basis. Otherwise, students will think the odds are in their favor, and their misbehavior is not likely to be punished. When you tell a student he will be disciplined, you must follow through.

Following through is easy to do if the penalty is immediately leveled, such as putting his name on the board. He knows he will have to stay after class, and the name on the board is a reminder for you. However, if the penalty is to occur the next day, such as a detention to be served or a special assignment to be turned in, you are liable to forget. To help you to remember, write a note to yourself and stick it on your computer monitor or in your plan book. Just put it somewhere where you will be sure to see it.

What to Say When Disciplining Students

When you are addressing students about their behavior, come right to the point. Students don't need or want to be lectured about their shortcomings; just tell them what they did wrong and what the consequence of their misbehavior will be. Choose your words so that students will stop misbehaving without becoming embarrassed or angry. The following sections explain how to accomplish this feat.

Letting Students Decide Their Own Fate

Nobody likes to be told what to do. Individuals would rather feel they had a say in what happens to them. So, when leveling discipline measures, give students a choice. Instead of saying, "Since you won't be quiet while the lesson is being taught, you sit over here," try giving the student some control over the situation by saying, *"Would you rather sit where you are and pay attention to the lesson or move to this seat where you will have no one to talk to?"*

Once you think in terms of offering the student choices, phrasing your disciplinary talk in these terms becomes easy. Here are some common uses of this technique:

> *"Would you rather listen to my directions now or have me repeat them to you after class?"*

> *"Would you rather work during class or during Saturday School?"*

> *"Would you like to be quiet now or sit quietly in this room for a couple of minutes after the bell rings?*

> *"Would you like to continue working in groups or work silently on the project by yourself?"*

> *"Would you like to work quietly on this assignment in class now or have it as homework?"*

Be sure that every option you offer is one that you are ready to put into effect immediately. Don't give your students a choice and then not honor their request.

Using Positive Language

When speaking to a student who is misbehaving, make it clear what you want done. Use sentences beginning with words such as *"I want you to…,"* *"I need you to…,"* or *" I expect you to…."* Emphasize the positive rather than the negative. Phrasing your admonishments with words like "Stop doing that" or beginning a sentence with "Don't" may cause a student to snap back with "I wasn't doing anything," "It wasn't me," or "It wasn't my fault."

If the problem centers on a student not doing schoolwork, try saying, *"May I help you with your assignment?"* *"May I show you how to get started?"* or *"How's your paper coming?"* rather than "Why aren't you working?" or "Let's get to work."

Focusing on the Behavior, Not the Student

You would be surprised at how many students think that when you discipline them, it means you don't like them. Many students actually have to hear you say, *"I like you. It is your behavior I don't like."* As a teacher you have to remind yourself of this point as well, because it's hard to be an effective teacher if you don't like your students. Usually if you can get past their disruptive antics, you will find that students are pretty endearing.

> **TIP** Once in a while there comes along a student you just can't like. Accept this. Go out of your way to treat this student fairly and continue to be friendly.

Forgiving students when they misbehave is important. Every day each student should start with a clean slate; what happened yesterday shouldn't be held against her today. If you discipline a student one day, let her know you don't hold grudges by giving her a smile, having a friendly conversation with her, or sharing a joke with her the next day. Students need reassurance that you still care about them.

Most school years there will be one class that you dread, a group of little demons that appears before you each day like an omen telling you that you should have followed your inclination years ago to sell insurance. This group excels in annoying behavior and has elevated obnoxiousness to an art form. No matter how much you are bothered by these students, you have to make the best of this situation and not let them know how you feel. Kids are experts at reading facial expressions and body language; they know when you don't like them. Here again, make sure they all understand that it's their behavior you don't like, not them as individuals. If you adopt this attitude, you'll find that even these kids are likeable.

Don't Take Away Their Dignity

Kids are proud. To be dressed down or yelled at by a teacher in front of their peers humiliates them. Rather than "lose face," they may react to you by talking back, smirking, or walking out of the class. They will do whatever it takes to preserve their dignity.

Make sure your comments address the problem rather than attacking the character of the student. Show respect for the student. Don't belabor the issue. Get the situation corrected and then continue with the lesson. Remember that while you may be focused on a particular student, the rest of the class is watching you. Don't give them a reason to sympathize with the student you are disciplining. Be the good guy.

First-Response Techniques for Classroom Control

Some classroom control techniques have been around as long as there have been teachers. When you are trying to teach a lesson or lead a discussion, try these techniques when the first signs of misbehavior appear:

- **Give them the pause.** Stop what you are doing. The absence of your voice signals a change, and the room will become unnaturally quiet. The conversation that was running while you were talking also stops or suddenly becomes so obvious that everyone hears the talkers. They will usually stop in mid-sentence. This technique also quiets the pencil tappers, toe tappers, and chair squeakers.

- **Apply the look.** This technique is often used in combination with the pause because when you stop talking, everyone, including the misbehavers, looks your way. When their eyes meet your stare, they usually comply with your wishes. You don't have to glare at them; just a quizzical or even a friendly look will usually get their cooperation. Save the evil eye for the chronic disruptors.

- **Lower your voice.** You may not be the only one talking in your classroom. Especially during activity times, you may find yourself trying to talk over the voices of several students. To make yourself heard, you invariably will talk louder. Instead, try lowering your voice and speaking more softly. Your students, no longer able to hear you, will become quiet.

I discovered this technique years ago when I had laryngitis and my voice was only a whisper. That day my students didn't dare make a sound as they strained to hear what I was saying. I learned then that if what you are saying is important to the class, they will quiet down to hear your words.

- **Walk toward trouble.** While still carrying on with the lesson, walk toward the students who are misbehaving. They will fall silent. Stand by them until they lose the impulse to talk.

- **Show them the stop sign.** Sometimes it is hard to make eye contact with the students who are causing the problem, or the students don't realize that what they are doing is wrong. In these situations, hold your hand out toward them and either point to them or show them the face of your hand in a stop gesture. Try to be as subtle as possible so that only the misbehaving student gets the signal.

- **Tap them back to attention.** When those disturbing the class are not facing you or don't see you approaching, tap them gently on the shoulder to get their attention.

> T I P Don't use this tap technique with volatile students or other students who might be upset if you touch them. Instead, lightly tap on their desk or table with a pencil or just reach over and briefly place your finger on the table or desk surface in front of them.

- **Involve them in the lesson.** Another trick that works well, especially during a discussion, is to direct questions toward individuals whose attention is lapsing or who are talking. Asking them a question forces them to focus on you and redirect their train of thought. You might also ask them to repeat the point or statement that you had just made in class. Hearing their names suddenly spoken forces them to reconnect with the lesson as they try to figure out why you mentioned their names.

TIP   If a student is daydreaming, make up a nonsensical or humorous question, direct it toward her, and ask, "Isn't that right?" She will usually say, "Yes," which will make the rest of the class laugh. The student will then try to pay attention. Only do this with students who will not be embarrassed.

If these gentle reminders don't work, it's time to implement strategies that involve disciplining the student.

What Every Adolescent Hates

So you've been pausing, giving them the look, walking toward them, waving hand signals, and tapping on their shoulders, but they're still not cooperating. It's time to give your students reasons to behave. Inform them that if they misbehave, unpleasant things will happen to them.

Adolescents fear loss of free time, separation from friends, and negative peer response. When teachers focus on these fears, students will behave. Let's examine these fears in a bit more detail.

- **Loss of free time.** If you keep a student after class for a few minutes, you have taken away some of his free time. The threat of having to stay even a minute after class will tame most youth. The most important people to them are their peers. If students sit in class for a minute while their classmates are milling in the hall between classes, they are miserable.

- **Separation from friends.** For students, the best place to be in a classroom is near their friends. If given the option of choosing their own seats, they will plunk themselves down next to their buddies. The threat of losing their seats and being moved next to people they don't know and who aren't cool is a powerful incentive to behave.

- **Negative peer response.** Though families are important to kids and they may like teachers, the center of kids' existence, beginning in their preteen years, is their peers. Their social goal in life is to be accepted by their peers. They will do almost anything to be liked by their classmates and will tailor their classroom behavior to meet this need. Knowing this, a teacher can sometimes get kids to behave by helping them to act in a way to avoid receiving a negative peer response.

Realizing that kids don't want to lose their free time, change seats, or be in disfavor with their peers enables teachers to establish effective classroom management plans. The next three chapters explain exactly how to implement these plans.

Summary

Managing student behavior involves defining misbehavior, taking action, and understanding your students. This chapter introduced a basic framework for a system of classroom control. By using the techniques presented in this chapter, you can help your class accept your discipline plan without resentment.

Keep the following main points in mind:

- Don't get bogged down in classroom rules. Just make it clear that students who prevent you from teaching effectively will be disciplined.

- When you discipline students, try to phrase the consequences as a choice. Use positive language, and comment only on the behavior, not on the student as a person.

- Use first-response techniques such as pausing to let misbehaving students know that you notice what they are doing. These techniques are effective in stopping minor misbehavior such as talking without causing a major disruption.

- The three most effective penalties for kids are loss of free time, separation from friends, and negative peer response.

CHAPTER 2

Using the Stay-After-Class Threat Effectively

Pavlov was right! Dogs can be conditioned. And so can students. Anyone who ever takes a high school psychology course learns about Ivan Pavlov, the Russian physiologist who rang a bell when he fed his dogs. Knowing food was coming when the bell was rung, the dogs salivated. Soon the dogs would salivate at the sound of the bell; food was no longer needed to stimulate them. Kids respond just as eagerly as Pavlov's dogs, but you don't need a bell for kids; a marker will do fine.

Let me explain. Whereas Pavlov's dogs hungered for food, students hunger for freedom. At the end of class, they want out. To have to stay even one minute after the period finishes is torture. When students misbehave, the teacher indicates who has to stay after class by writing the students' names on the board. If you use this system consistently, you can stop misbehavior just by picking up a marker and walking toward the board.

This chapter explains how to use the names-on-the-board system effectively and handle the issues that arise when you have to keep students after class as punishment. In cases where the threat of staying after class does not stop misbehavior, the threat of detention after school might. This chapter explains the role of detention in classroom discipline as well.

Names on the Board

Writing names of talkers and disruptors on the board has probably been used since the days of the one-room school, but it works. The names-on-the-board system is designed to quell minor disruptions such as kids talking, making noises (moving chairs, crinkling paper, tapping pencils), interrupting you, or being out of their seats. The students whose names are written on the board have to stay one to three minutes after class.

Seeing names of their classmates on the board stifles others' impulse to misbehave. When you write a student's name on the board, you make sure that the offender knows he's in trouble and let the rest of the class know that they, too, had better shape up or their names may be added to the list. Of course, no system is perfect. There are strategies you will need to use to make this system work for you and to handle students who try to defeat the system.

How Can I Make This System Work in My Classroom?

There is a trick to using the names-on-the-board system effectively. Your goal should be to get to a point where you don't have to write any names on the board. I wrote the names of disruptive students on the board and kept those students after class from the beginning of the year. When I wrote the names, I always picked up the marker, lifted it a little more dramatically than normal, and then wrote the name of the disruptor on a specific place on the board.

I followed exactly the same procedure every time, although I might write more than one name at a time. By the second or third week of the school year, the students were so conditioned that when I picked up the marker, turned to the board, and started to print a letter, a hush descended over the room. A month into the year, just picking up the marker quieted the room.

When I wrote a name, I would not usually comment. I would just continue teaching. If the student asked how long he had to stay after class,

I would say, *"It depends on how well the rest of the period goes."* If a student asked what having her name on the board meant, I would just say, *"We'll talk about that after class."* After awhile, no one said anything when I put his or her name on the board.

Keep these pointers in mind when you write students' names on the board:

- Always use the same spot on the board for writing the names of misbehaving students. That way, the class will become conditioned to know that when you move in that direction, the disciplinary ax may fall.

- Make a point of picking up the marker from the tray and moving to the place on the board that you always write the names of those you catch misbehaving. If you consistently use the same procedures to write names on the board, your students will learn these nonverbal cues and curb their behavior.

- Sometimes when you've allowed several minor disruptions to go on without correcting them, you may have to verbally tell the

The "Three, Two" Technique

You're in the back of the room at your desk taking attendance at the beginning of the hour and your class, whose backs are turned to you, talks louder and louder. Or you're up front leading a spirited discussion that is getting out of control. In either case you're not sure that just picking up a marker and walking toward the board will get your students settled down, at least not right away. So you say "Three, two," and they fall silent. Some may continue to speak, but they are now looking at you. When you pick up the marker, the class becomes quiet.

I picked up this technique from a fellow teacher, and it works. This teacher noticed that in a television studio when they are about to go on the air, the director counts "three, two" and silently mouths "one," and the cameras roll. This is to cue all in the studio that they must be quiet or their voices will be heard on the air. This teacher brought the idea to his classroom, explained its meaning, and now gets the class quiet with a simple command of "three, two."

class that you are about to write names on the board. If your students fall silent after that pronouncement, you don't need to write names.

- When you put names on the board, don't tell the students how long they will have to stay after class. By hinting that the number of minutes they stay depends on how they behave the rest of the class period, you will pretty much guarantee that they will behave well and pay attention for the remainder of the class period.

- At the end of the hour, make sure that all those with their names on the board stay after class. The system doesn't work if you don't follow through with the punishment.

What If Students Want Their Names on the Board?

Expect that at some point a student will say to you, "I like to have my name on the board," or "Please put my name on the board." Such a statement is obviously an attention-getting ploy done to win peer approval and to put you on the spot.

Don't react or comment. If you had already written her name on the board, leave it there. If the student's name isn't on the board, don't write it there unless her statement about wanting her name on the board creates a disruption in the class. Instead, continue with your lesson. Don't give these students the reaction or attention they are seeking.

What If a Student Refuses to Stay After Class?

If a student whose name was on the board takes off after class instead of staying, assume he forgot about it and remind him of this the next day, pointing out that he now will have to stay two days. Be sure and make a note of this, so you don't forget to remind him to stay the second day.

However, if the student skips out on the next day or says, "I am not going to stay after class," respond calmly by telling him you need to see him after class. At the end of class, as students are leaving, walk over to the misbehaver without being obvious and quietly say you need to talk to him. Because the student may want to play to an audience, speak to him so you can't be overheard saying, *"You have a choice: You can stay now for two minutes or receive a detention. What would you prefer, two minutes now or an hour after school?"* Go with the student's decision. With no peers to impress, the student invariably takes the two-minute penalty.

What If Students Complain That They Will Be Late for Their Next Class?

Occasionally a student will complain that if she stays after class she will be late to her next class. To deal with this issue, walk with a student, preferably the complainer, to the faraway classroom. As you leave your room, click on the stopwatch function on your wristwatch or just check the time on the dial. Note how long it takes you to get from place to place. Then you and that student will know how long it takes to cover the distance. Because every year kids complain that they haven't enough time to get to that distant classroom, you will be able to tell students for the rest of your teaching career how long they can stay after class and still not be late after you note the travel time once.

The Role of Detentions in Discipline

Handing out detentions is the logical thing to do once you have exhausted all your in-class options for handling disruption. The downside is that when you resort to issuing detentions, you are becoming reliant on the system to bail you out. Typically once you write a detention, the slip goes to the office where the student is then assigned to stay an hour after school.

Although virtually every staff person occasionally finds reason to give detentions, the following problems occur when a teacher issues detentions frequently:

- The paperwork takes time to complete. Usually while the teacher is writing up the student, the rest of the class is no longer under direct supervision and may take the opportunity to cause mischief.

- Overuse of detentions causes students to lose their respect for the detention as a punishment. The students may also start to suspect that the teacher is not able to control the class without relying on detentions.

- Detentions often require follow-up, which may take the teacher away from the class or use after-school time. Some schools require a phone call with every detention issued, and the detention form itself may be extensive and require additional record keeping.

- Administrators may doubt the teacher's ability to manage the class if they see numerous detentions from that teacher.

How to Use Detentions as Attention Getters

When you rarely give detentions, it enhances their value as a deterrent. One day when my class just couldn't seem to get it together, I walked to the front of the room and taped a blank detention slip to the front of the board. I then announced, in a sharper tone of voice than usual, that the next student who disturbed the class would receive that detention slip. Because I rarely give detentions, the students were somewhat intimidated and settled down immediately. Seeing that detention slip taped to the board served as a reminder to behave well.

Occasionally I have simply pulled a blank detention slip from my desk and held it while I presented a lesson. It has an effect not unlike that when someone pulls out a gun on a TV program. Everyone suddenly becomes more cooperative.

I know a teacher who kept only detention slips in one drawer. The kids knew what was coming when she reached for that drawer. After awhile all she had to do to restore classroom order was extend her hand toward that drawer.

For the most part, the detention was rarely seen or used in my class-room, so when it became part of the scene, it got everyone's attention. When I threatened to use a detention, the odds were good that I wouldn't have to actually issue one.

When Detentions Aren't Deterrents

Although most kids want to avoid detentions, others appear to be unaffected by them. To them another hour in school isn't a big deal. Staying after school may allow them to miss out on chores at home or avoid having to ride the bus. It may be a show of bravado on their part to impress their classmates. They may react with words to the effect of "Detentions don't bother me."

To this retort, respond by calmly saying in your normal tone of voice, *"I'd like to talk to you after class,"* and then move on with your

The Detention Bomb

Kenny was a likable eighth grader who never caused major problems, yet he could hardly sit still. He would often talk or push on the seat in front of him while I was talking. Keeping him quiet and focused on the lesson was a challenge. Disciplining Kenny was also hard because he was funny and personable.

One day he was being his usual busy and distracting self while I was conducting class. Impulsively I grabbed a blank detention form, slapped it on his desk, and then smiled at him and said, "Kenny, have you ever seen one of those movies where someone is tied to a bomb and is told that any movement he makes will set off the bomb? Well, this detention slip is like a bomb, and if you distract this class in any way, this detention slip will be activated." Kenny looked startled and then smiled; he also remained perfectly behaved throughout the hour. At the end of the period, I collected the blank detention slip.

I would never do something like that on a regular basis, because it would soon become a joke. And I would never do that with a kid who was a hardcore troublemaker or who didn't have a sense of humor. But with a kid like Kenny it was fun, and he enjoyed playing the game that hour. And most importantly, I was able to teach in a quieter classroom.

lesson. Be sure you don't challenge the student by saying something like, "We'll see about that," or just handing him the detention slip. He may then go a step farther by tearing it up. Seeing the student after the class robs him of his peer group audience and enables you to figure out whether his cavalier attitude toward the detention was a bluff or true indifference.

When the class period ends and the students leave, fill out the detention form, hand it to the student, and say, *"I would like you to serve this detention, and I hope it never becomes necessary to give you another one."* He may still exhibit bravado and act as if it doesn't bother him.

Later check with the staff person who monitors the after-school detention and ask him or her to note the student's reaction when he serves the detention. If he isn't fazed by spending time after school, you'll have to adjust your behavior plan for this student. One option might be a seating change; having to relocate may be enough of a penalty to change his behavior. On the other hand, the likelihood is that although the student may not mind staying after school, he doesn't relish being detained during school hours. Try keeping him for a couple minutes after your class ends for several consecutive days or arranging to spend part of a lunch period with him.

A call home may settle the issue, especially if the student hopes to get a ride home with parents instead of having to sit on the school bus or is missing out on chores when he is held after class. Calling the parent and discussing the student's attitude toward after-school time may give you some insights into why the student doesn't see detentions as a penalty. It may also be that the parents will become your allies in getting their child to behave better.

Summary

Remember that the goal of classroom discipline is to control your students' behavior so that you can teach effectively. You don't want to spend a lot of time as a teacher writing names on the board, keeping students after class, and filling out detention slips. Keep the ideas in this chapter in mind when you threaten students with the loss of free time:

- Staying after class and serving detention are effective punishments because most adolescents hate to give up their free time.

- By using the names-on-the-board system consistently, you can condition your class to settle down when you pick up a marker and walk to the board.

- Avoid giving detentions if at all possible. Often just the threat of detentions is enough to regain control of the classroom.

CHAPTER 3

Making Seat Assignments

If the most effective way to gain student cooperation results from threatening or actually taking away free time, changing a seat ranks a close second. Most students know where they want to be and whom they want next to them, yet the teacher controls the seating plan. Intelligent use of this power brings harmony to the classroom. Getting the best seating arrangement without appearing to be an autocrat is an art. This chapter will help you become the artist.

Choosing a Location for Your Desk

The first seat you should assign is your own. Depending on your teaching style, your desk may function as the command center, a storage area, or a refuge. There may even be times when you would like to hide under it. How you use your desk has a lot to do with where you put it.

If you like to sit or stand behind your desk when you deliver the lesson, then of course your desk should be at the front of the room. Seated here at your desk you can see every face, and students can see you. The disadvantage to this desk location is that your class will also know when you are not watching. Any time that the class sees you reading or assisting a student will become an opportunity for students to misbehave.

Setting your desk between the door and where your students sit is a mistake because every time classes change you will feel like you are parked on a highway median. In addition, every student who enters or leaves the room during the class period will parade by your desk, which will be annoying if you are seated there or standing behind it trying to teach. The more creative of your charges may pause as they slip into class to entertain the class with a mime routine behind your back.

> **TIP** Positioning your desk so that you can see out the door enables you to see would-be entertainers roaming in the hall.

A desk positioned in the back or off to the side of the room allows you to see the side or back of every student. This desk position makes it harder for students to fool around because they never can be sure whether you are watching them. You will spend less time at your desk when it is in the back of the room because it's necessary to be in front of your students when you do most of your teaching.

Implementing the Seating Chart

In an ideal world, seating charts would be necessary only for taking attendance. Junior high kids certainly don't want them. They would rather sit with their friends who have much more to offer than what you are teaching. Consequently, if the first thing you do at the beginning of the school year is stand everyone up and then point each kid to his assigned seat, you are not winning any friendship points.

Instead, observe your students the first day as they enter the classroom, noting how they choose where to sit. Some, seeing a friend enter, gesture frantically for him or her to sit near them. You may even see someone get shooed out of a seat so that someone else can have that seat. Just watching kids select their seats can tell you a lot about the social hierarchy of junior high.

The standard self-chosen eighth grade seating chart looks like this: in the back, in the farthest corner away from the teacher's desk at the front of the room, are three to five guys. These guys have about as much chance of behaving as raccoons in a garbage can. Then there will be several girls clustered together; they may whisper or giggle some and often are fanatical note writers. Usually there are a couple guys whose worlds revolve around video games or cars; other than occasionally trying to read a trade magazine while you are teaching, they tend to be pretty cooperative. Scattered about the room are some students who are seriously immature and will manage to antagonize anyone near them. These kids are eager to socialize but are clueless when it comes to sensitivity to others. The rest of the class are just kids who want to stay out of trouble; some actually want to do well in your class, and a few just want to be left alone—passing your course is not one of their priorities. All these kids choose their seats, and they don't want to move.

I explained to my students that they would get to choose the first seating chart and I would make the second one. Soon after the first day of school, I told them to come in the next day and pick the seats they would like to have for the rest of the year. After everyone sat down in a seat the following day, I reminded the students that this was their last chance to choose. Usually at that point there was some frantic, last-minute scurrying around. After everyone found a chair, I penciled in the seating chart.

Typically I would have 30 desks in my classroom, and all but a couple were occupied. As a result, if I had to change a seat, not only would the misbehaving student have to move, but he also would exchange seats with a student who wasn't causing any problems. Knowing this, I would give my seating chart spiel:

"I'm glad everyone's settled. I think it's important to be near your friends, but remember I have to teach, and anything that interferes with my ability to teach or your ability to learn is a problem." The students were already familiar with that idea because I stressed it the

day before in my opening talk with them about my discipline philosophy. I continued, *"If I feel where you are seated is a problem, I will move you and give you a new permanent seat. I don't feel sorry for you because you, by your behavior, made the move necessary. However, I do feel sorry for the person who has to lose his seat so you can have a new place to sit. He did nothing wrong, and now because of your behavior he must move to your seat."* By saying this, I hoped students realized that having their seat changed not only cost them a chance to sit with their friends, but also created some peer resentment toward them.

Changing the Seating Chart

During the first few days with the student-chosen seating chart, avoid moving anyone. Address behavior problems by telling the disruptive

Alphabetical Seating Charts

Some teachers favor using an alphabetized seating chart. In this classic method of student placement, the As sit in the front, and the Zs occupy the back seats. Unlike the penciled-in chart described in this chapter that changes many times, the alphabetical chart can be written in ink. The advantage comes when collecting and handing out papers. Because student grade lists are alphabetized, if the seat chart is done in a like manner, distribution of student work is greatly simplified. Another plus to this system is that a permanent seating chart is much easier for the teacher to memorize, and it pretty much kills the excuse of "I forgot where my seat is" after the first week.

The disadvantage to an alphabetical seating chart is that students may not like where they are assigned and may actually misbehave in hopes of being seated somewhere else. Also, most teachers who use the A to Z plan have to make occasional changes to accommodate the nearsighted and especially unruly students. These variations in alphabetical order lessen the advantages of an alphabetical system. In contrast, if teachers let students initially select their seat assignments, the students have some ownership in where they are sitting, which gives them an incentive to behave so they can remain there.

student that if the problem surfaces again she will lose her seat. Let students know it isn't your fault that they have to change seats; it's their choice. Making this idea clear will increase the students' support of your class rules, and this support is vital to successful class management. Ideally when you discipline a student, the class feels that disciplining the student is the fair and right thing to do.

Some seating charts remain virtually unchanged; with others you're constantly erasing and shifting names. It can become like a chess game as you move students trying to find a combination that gains you the chance to teach without disruption. The guys in the back corner invariably go first, shifted to seats where their social nature is stifled by being placed among quiet, studious types. To fill the empty seats, you have to select girls. If you put other boys back there, they'll either join in on the fun with the guys or be persecuted by them. Taking one nice, quiet girl and dropping her back next to those guys seems unfair. Instead, I suggest moving two girls who are friends to the back of the class so they won't feel alone among the now subdued remnants of the boys' social club.

Then there's the kid who pokes people, grabs their stuff, fidgets, talks, and just annoys anyone sitting next to him. Nobody wants to sit near this kid. This one gets the "branch office," a desk off in a corner where he is a part of the class but can't physically touch anyone. This is one seat that students can work their way out of with good behavior. When assigned to the branch office, most kids clean up their act hoping to get another chance to sit close to their peers.

Some kids just have short attention spans; they need constant reminders about getting down to work, paying attention, and being quiet while people are talking. Changing their seats doesn't alter their behavior because it isn't specific people that get them going, it is just their nature. They usually wind up in a seat that is near your desk or the front of the room where you do most of your teaching. By being near you, they are more receptive to picking up a cue such as a look, a hand signal, a slight shake of the head, or just a movement in their

Study Carrel Fiasco

Earlier in my teaching career, I thought that maybe my discipline problems would disappear if the troublemakers literally disappeared from view. Deciding that some students preferred doing time in the hall to doing time in my class, I managed to procure an old study carrel that was orphaned from the library during renovation. I also reasoned that students in the study carrel wouldn't miss out on the lesson because they could still hear me teaching. If a student disrupted the class, he was assigned to the study carrel, which the students immediately dubbed "the box."

This experiment yielded mixed results. Some students assigned to the box did their work and stayed silent; others realized because they were not visible to the rest of us that they could sleep, draw, or do just about anything without being disturbed. Because the top of the box was higher than students could reach, raising a hand to ask or answer a question was impossible, until the day a student brought a glove to class, hung it on a ruler, and raised it over the top of the box. After that, the box became kind of a game room where students wanted to be so that they could come up with a new way to disrupt class. The study carrel soon exited the room never to be seen again.

direction. This nearness means that you don't have to stop the lesson to correct a problem. You can deal with it in a subtle way without the class being aware of it.

Even after you have carefully rearranged the students into a workable seating chart, certain situations will occur that will make you question the seating chart all over again.

When Students Sit in the Wrong Seats

Sometimes students will drop down in a new seat when you're not watching. You have to deal with this issue. If you don't, everyone will want to change seats.

When you see students who have shifted seats, ask them to return to their correct seats, and then announce that if it happens again the seat-changers may be subjected to disciplinary action, which usually means having the student stay a minute or two after class. Another technique, which works well when you are taking attendance, is to look at the empty seat and call the student's name. The "absent" individual will usually move into his seat before you can mark him absent.

Sometimes you won't be aware of seat changes until several students have moved. On one occasion when I realized that several students had switched seats, I covered my eyes and said, *"I'm going to count to five, and when I uncover my eyes, there will be a surprise for everyone who is in the wrong seat."* All the relocated students scurried back to their home seats before I reached the count of five. You might think that covering eyes and counting to five sounds a little childish for junior high, but if you do it in a lighthearted manner, students think it is fun, and it accomplishes the task.

When You Can't Change a Student's Seat

Kurt was a popular student who needed constant reminders about socializing with his seatmates. Changing his seat seemed like a good option, except his nearsightedness meant that he needed to sit where he could see the board. His class had so many gregarious students that any seating arrangement I could concoct still left talkers near one another.

Kurt knew I couldn't change his seat, so he continued to talk until I made this statement to him: *"Kurt, the next time I find you talking to your friends, I will change their seats."* His friends, all of whom liked where they were sitting, started shushing Kurt and telling him not to talk to them any more. Kurt and his cronies suddenly became a much quieter clan.

When Students Want Their Seats Back

Sometimes a student asks to get her seat back. Depending on the circumstances, you might agree to honor her request. I suggest telling the student that you will monitor her behavior for a week. If things go well, she can return to her original seat. If the student behaves well and moves back to her original seat, make sure she understands that there will be no second chances. If she screws up again, she will lose her seat permanently.

Keep up mind that if you give one student a chance to return to her original seat, every other student who ever had his seat changed will want a second chance as well. Tell students that you will see how the first student's trial period works and then you will look at more changes. This statement buys you some time and puts a little more pressure on the student wanting the seat change to behave.

Using the Seating Chart to Improve Academic Performance

As I said earlier, in a perfect world there would be no seating charts, and junior high is a far from perfect world. Because where students sit is an important part of their social lives, you can use the seating chart as an incentive to not only change their behavior, but also to improve their work in school.

Improving Grades

Once you have established a seating chart, students will want to make changes. This bid to relocate can be a bartering chip for improving grades. It works something like this:

"Mr. Foley, can I sit next to Paul?"

"John, you and Paul are such good friends that I'm afraid you wouldn't be paying attention while I'm teaching. After all, I think you're getting a C in this class, and I know you can do better."

"Honest, we'll be good, and I'll get all my work in on time."

"I'll tell you what. If you can raise your grade to B, I'll let you move over next to Paul as long as you don't disturb class and don't let your grade slip below a B. I also expect Paul to continue to do good work and behave as well."

This strategy usually works. John now has an incentive to work harder and behave in class. If Paul's behavior or academic performance dips, then his seat is in jeopardy.

A variation of this situation occurs when a good student and a not-so-good student who are friends sit together. For example, Jane, an *A* student, sits next to Jill, who is just an average student. What frequently happens in this instance is that Jane finishes her work and then distracts Jill.

You can usually remedy this problem by telling Jane that she will have to take another seat if Jill's grades drop even a little bit. From then on, typically you'll find Jane becoming an academic mentor to Jill so that they can continue to sit together. The end result is that Jane continues to earn good grades while Jill's work improves significantly.

Motivating Students

Some students refuse to try. You carefully explain a problem and then have the students work on an example. One student just sits there. You ask if she needs help, and her reply is, "I don't get it." "I don't get it," or "No," is her answer to every question you ask her. From past experience you know the student is capable of doing the work, but she is just refusing to try.

Shauna was just such a student for me. During an exercise on finding verbs, for example, the dialogue would go something like this:

"Shauna, can I help you?"

"I don't get this."

"Can you tell what the verb is in this sentence?" I would ask, pointing to a short sentence where the verb is easy to find.

"No." This answer was surprising because Shauna had found verbs successfully in the past.

"Can you tell me what a verb is?"

"No." Again this answer was surprising because Shauna and the rest of the class knew how to identify verbs.

"Okay, then do you know what the subject of this sentence is?"

"No."

By this time the rest of the class was done with the exercise, and I had to begin going over it with them. I was sure Shauna understood the lesson, so the first chance I had I returned to where she was sitting and told her I wanted to give her some special help. To do this I was going to change her seat back near my desk where I could help her. Because she was sitting in a seat she had chosen near her friends, she didn't want to move. However, I insisted on the move.

The next day she "miraculously" knew what verbs were and could readily identify them. She also asked to return to her old seat. I indicated that if at the end of the week she was still doing well, she could have her old seat back.

When a good student claims she can't understand the material, assigning her a seat near your desk often provides the impetus she needs to put forth some effort. It also enables you to give her additional help, because you can easily check her progress without constantly having to hover over her desk. Invariably she will work hard to succeed so she can return to her original seat.

Summary

Creating a seating arrangement that works for both you and your students doesn't just happen. Like skilled chess players, most veteran teachers are able to move students about until a winning combination is found. By using the strategies described in this chapter, you also can establish a seating chart that minimizes disruption.

Keep the following points in mind:

- Carefully consider the best location for your desk. Think about how you use your desk in your teaching and the fact that you need to be able to closely monitor disruptive students.

- Students want to sit next to their friends, which is why the threat of seat changes is an effective deterrent to bad behavior. In order to use this threat effectively, you need to let students choose where they sit at first.

- Throughout the year, you will need to move students to different seats in order to separate talkers, isolate disruptors from the rest of the class, and encourage students to improve their academic performance.

Using Peer Pressure to Improve Behavior

As students enter junior high, being accepted by their peers becomes exceedingly important to them. Although they may still respond to adults, they are less likely to be teacher pleasers or devoted to their parents. Oftentimes they are driven to act out in order to win favor among their peer group. If the group approves, then the acting out continues. However, any behavior that elicits a negative reaction of the peer group will be extinguished.

If a student does not respond to your efforts to get him to behave, then consider getting the student's classmates to give the message that they don't condone that behavior either. This chapter explains how peer pressure can help you solve classroom management problems.

Identifying the Unseen Disruptor

You're leading a discussion when a paper wad arcs across the room or a spitball thuds into the blackboard. Looking toward the general area where the missile might have originated, you see nothing but cherubic faces. If it's obvious that you saw the flying object, remark that the activity cannot be repeated and that you will have to deal with it if it happens again. Then continue with your discussion. You are hoping another object won't be thrown because stopping to deal with the problem may cause you to lose the momentum of the discussion you were conducting at that time.

If another paper wad or spitball flies after you have given a warning, you must address the situation. Begin by looking over to where the problem started, and ask the thrower to identify himself. Because you indicated earlier that throwing things was not allowed and then another item was thrown, the class understands why you must deal with the offender. Hopefully, the student identifies himself, and then you put his name on the board to stay after class.

If no one comes forward, then ask a group of three to five students, sitting near where the toss originated, to stay after class. Ask again for the thrower to identify himself, saying that if he identifies himself now the penalty will be just a few minutes after class. Explain that if he doesn't reveal himself, these students will have to stay after class for a couple of minutes. You can be sure that if several innocent parties have to stay after class, they and the whole class will be unhappy with the culprit. No kid wants the disfavor of his peers, and if he allows others to go down with him, the paper thrower will gain disfavor. Invariably the guilty party, not wanting to alienate his peers, will admit to being the thrower and stay alone after class.

> T I P   In addition to dealing with students who throw objects, you can also use this strategy when faced with someone talking under their breath, whistling, or making a noise such as tapping or clicking.

The Peer Pressure Confession

Suppose you hear the clack of a small object ricocheting off the back wall, followed almost immediately by a voice saying, "Someone threw this at me." As you turn from the board where you had been writing, you see Janet holding up a small plastic pen top. Throwing things in class isn't allowed; you have to respond to this incident.

Start by admonishing the class by saying something like, *"Someone could have been hurt, and you know throwing stuff disrupts class,"* and then ask, *"Will the person who threw the pen top please tell me*

© JIST Works

who you are?" Note that all your comments are geared toward convincing the thrower to confess. Individual students will rarely willingly tell on another student because they don't want the class to view them as snitches.

If no one says a thing, remind the class that there must be consequences for disrupting the lesson. For example, say, *"This has happened before, and the thrower has been disciplined. It wouldn't be fair to just let someone get away with this. I don't think I should just ignore this."* Look and listen to the class for signs of support, such as head nods and positive murmurs. Continue by saying, *"I know some of you saw the pen top being thrown. I want the thrower to identify himself now, or the whole class will stay three minutes after class."* When you have class support in a situation that everyone can see is wrong, and several members of the class know who caused the problem, the threat of punishing the class will lead to a resolution of the problem.

> T I P   Before you threaten to keep the entire group after class, be sure that several students witnessed the misbehavior.

At this point, several hands should go up. You may even hear mumbled threats. In junior high, as soon as something threatens to inconvenience students, the hallowed "no snitch" rule is abandoned. Give the thrower one last chance to confess by saying, *"Wait, please be quiet, we still have to finish the lesson. The only person I need to hear from is the thrower."* In most cases, the culprit will confess, realizing no punishment you could levy could be as unpleasant as being ostracized by his peers. When you receive an admission of guilt, thank the student for being honest and having the integrity to admit the deed.

The Perils of Punishing the Whole Class

Although you might threaten to have the entire class stay in their seats after the period ends, this threat should only be tried when you have

Behave, the Camera Is Watching

In the 1980s, video cameras were a novelty, and my school purchased a couple, one of which was a lemon. Nobody could get it to work. Seeing this camera gave me an idea. After school one night I installed it on a high shelf with its nonfunctioning lens pointed down on my classroom.

The next day I informed my classes that Michigan State University was making videos of junior high classrooms for a study on student misbehavior and adolescent immaturity. The camera they were looking at was programmed to film the class at various intervals throughout the day so that sometimes it would be on and sometimes it would be off. Even I didn't know when it would be operating. The next week one of their staff would be in to pick up the tape. People at the university would edit the tape so college students in psychology classes could study adolescent behavior.

The students accepted the camera and the fact that it had been rigged without lights so they would never know when it was operating. Not wanting to have their antics caught on tape, my students were angelic that week. If their behavior started to fray, I casually mentioned the camera and speculated if it was recording at that moment. I would see them quickly glance at the lens and then adopt an appropriate studious demeanor. Friday after school I took down the camera, figuring a week was about as long as I could continue the ruse.

a situation that must be resolved before the students leave the class. For example, when an item has been stolen, you might consider keeping the class after the bell. You might also use this option when an object has been thrown, and you realize many in the class know who did it, as was cited earlier.

If you do find yourself keeping the whole class back, it had better be a situation where everyone is guilty. Otherwise the well-behaved kids will feel, and rightly so, that they are being treated unfairly. In this situation, your popularity will drop. You are no longer the good guy if you are punishing the innocent.

Using the Three Strikes Technique

A class's level of cooperation often depends on what you're teaching. If students are having fun with the lesson, they don't want you to stop or switch to a less desirable activity. In this situation, all you have to do if they start misbehaving is to tell them that if they don't shape up, you will stop the fun, and they will do something else.

> **TIP** Generally the more structure there is in a lesson, the easier it is to keep the class behaved and on task. Most lessons can readily be changed to add more structure.

The three strikes technique works well in this case and gives the students a feeling of controlling their destiny. To use this technique, start by saying, *"The third time I have to stop teaching because of a disruption, we'll stop doing this."* Continue to teach, and when a problem occurs, say, *"That's one."* When it happens a third time, say, *"That's three. Now take out your grammar books (or whatever the backup plan is)."* You must follow through with your threat, so if you feel you absolutely must finish a lesson or reach a certain point before you stop, don't use the three strikes technique.

To make the three strikes ploy more effective, I sometimes introduced it to the class in a slightly different manner by telling them, *"The third time I have to stop teaching because of a disruption, I will indicate who caused the problem."* Thus when a problem occurred, I would say, *"Hannah's talking while I'm talking so that's strike one."* Now this comment made the class a bit more anxious, and they certainly weren't happy that Hannah caused them to get strike one. You can bet nobody wanted to be the cause of strike two or, worse yet, be the person named as the third strike. Once the class knew I would carry out my threat, we rarely got to strike three. The fear of peer disapproval was a strong incentive to behave.

I Will Not Make My Students Write Sentences

An older teacher convinced me that the way to get kids to stop misbehaving was to assign them sentences to write. He explained that nothing got better results with class talkers than having them write a hundred times. "I will not talk in class." So I tried it. Maybe if they wrote "I will not talk in class" a hundred times this idea would imprint on their brain and they would be quieter in class. This actually made sense to me, so you can see how desperate I was to get my classes to behave.

I would assign the sentences, and the students would turn them in the next day. I became skeptical of their ability to internalize the message when I saw that most kids would do the sentences vertically, writing "I, I, I, I, I, I, I" on the left side of the paper all the way to the bottom of the sheet, and then going to the top and writing "will, will, will, will, will, will, will, will" all the way down the page. They would continue a word at a time until the task was completed. To thwart this I learned to assign a sentence that was long enough so that it couldn't be written completely on one line. Now the kids had to write the penalty one sentence at a time.

I began to deviate from assigning the classic "I will not talk in class" or "I will not throw things in class" discipline sentences. Instead a student would find himself writing 25 copies of "I hate wasting my time writing this stupid sentence 25 times," or "Life is too short to spend it having to write a sentence as dumb as this one." Soon I figured out that having kids write sentences did little to change their behavior and was just a big waste of paper.

Presenting Options

You might hesitate to try the three strikes technique because you can't think of what your students would consider a fun activity. What you can do is give them options and watch them gravitate toward the "lesser evil."

For example, as a language arts teacher, I might say to the class, *"Today we can either read and analyze the poem 'The Raven' by Edgar Allen Poe or work on personal pronouns."* You can bet the class would clamor to study the poem; anything is more exciting than grammar. If I had not mentioned pronouns and instead just announced that we were reading "The Raven," there would have been groans.

> **T I P** The three strikes technique also works well when a lesson can be taught in different ways, such as either doing the work orally or writing it. Without doubt the students will opt for using their voices rather than their pencils, so that becomes the plan until the third strike, at which time the lesson becomes a written assignment.

Offering Incentives

Can you use the three strikes technique when you don't have a lesser evil? After all, you think, is there anything students dislike more than grammar? In that case, you offer them an incentive. You might say something like this:

"I know we're not fond of grammar, but it's something we all need in order for our written work to make sense, so here's what I propose. If you'll pay attention and help me work through this lesson, I'm willing to give you five minutes of free time at the end of class. However, the third time I have to stop class because of a disruption, you'll lose the free time and have to work right up until the bell rings."

Summary

When peer pressure is on your side, teaching becomes much easier. Using peer pressure is often the only option for settling problems when you are not sure who is causing the problem.

This chapter showed a couple of ways to use peer pressure to deal with classroom disruption:

- If you don't know who caused a disruption, threatening a group of students or even the whole class with punishment is an effective way to convince the culprit to confess. Most students would rather face punishment than make their peers angry with them.

- The three strikes technique works because no student wants to be the reason for the class to stop doing a fun activity, to switch to something boring, or to lose free time.

CHAPTER 5

Handling Common Problems

Trying to keep a class quiet and attentive is a never-ending task; it reminds me of weeding a garden. Even if you dutifully pull all the weeds in the garden each day, the next morning you'll find new weeds in your garden. Similarly with a classroom of kids, although you may have them perfectly under control one day, they'll come in ready to play around the next day if you don't continue to use effective classroom management techniques. This chapter provides solutions to the problems that crop up in every classroom.

Showing Off for the Class

Kids want to be noticed, so they show off for their classmates. Every class has a couple of comedians who will do anything for a laugh, and you are their straight man. They say funny things, make faces, drop things, and throw stuff, doing whatever they can to get a reaction out of you. These characters hope their antics provoke you enough that you will get mad, lose your temper, and yell at them. If you send them to the office or give them a detention, they become martyrs. If you show that you're embarrassed or act as though you are uncertain how to react, they like that, too.

These kids feel that if they upset you and provide the class with some entertainment at your expense, their popularity will soar. It's nothing personal against you. In most cases, they don't dislike you. However, their need for attention is so powerful that they will try whatever they think will entertain their peers or provide them with self-esteem by controlling your behavior.

The best reaction to this type of misbehavior is to barely acknowledge it. If it disrupts your class, use the subtlest means you can to quash the problem. Keep right on delivering your lesson and walk toward the problem area. Shoot a quick look at the perpetrators or ask them a question about the lesson. Try to end the mischief by not reacting to it.

If whatever happened disrupts the class and everybody's laughing, then just smile at the class and calmly say something like, *"Okay, let's move on."* Look at the student who caused the problem and, in a serious but even tone, state, *"We have work to do, and I need your help."* Don't wait for a response. Immediately continue the lesson. If something else happens, pick up a marker and put the disruptive student's name on the board.

Remember that the most successful class disruptions are a two-part drama consisting of the initial action followed by your reaction. You usually can't prevent the action, but you always can control your reaction. Follow these steps:

1. React as little as possible. Ignore the first disruption unless it's so obviously out of line that immediate action is needed.

2. Keep your voice calm. Don't yell or threaten.

3. Act quickly and decisively. For example, write the disruptive student's name on the board to stay after class. If the problem is way beyond usual classroom misbehavior, then you may need to assign detention or send the student to the office.

4. Return to the lesson.

For example, if I were joking with the class and conducting the lesson humorously, I may suddenly become all business with my teaching style when a student tries to disrupt the class. This change conveys the message that if a student disrupts the class, the class won't be able to have fun with the lesson.

When the class sees someone succeed in disrupting the classroom, other students will jump on the bandwagon and try their hand at being the class clowns. Be vigilant as you continue with the lesson. At every disruption, write the disruptor's name on the board. The class will soon be attentive and cooperative again.

Pulling Pranks and Playing Practical Jokes

For some students every day is April Fool's Day. When they are around, "Kick me" signs appear on backs, student notebooks wind up in the wastebasket, notes are written on the board, and paper confetti is sprinkled on people's hair. All of this nonsense is highly entertaining to junior high students, an age group whose standard for humor encompasses just about anything that isn't part of the daily routine. Your lesson plan just can't compete with a rubber snake that suddenly shows up on Danielle's desk.

If a prank occurs before you begin class or after you are done with the lesson, and it isn't mean-spirited or isn't going to hurt a student's feelings, you might just laugh with the class. Although enjoying a prank may help your students view you as less of a curmudgeon, it also may encourage the perpetrator or others to try further antics, because the purpose of most pranks is to gain attention.

The best approach is to point out that the prank disrupted class, making it difficult for you to teach and for the students to learn, thus the prankster needs to stay after class. If personal property was damaged or clean up is needed as a result of the prank, the prankster is responsible for that as well. In other words, everything must be returned to the way it was before the prank.

Of greater concern is the prank that has the potential of being injurious to the victim. Placing tacks on seats, pulling chairs out from under people, tripping students, and pushing students must be dealt with firmly. When an incident of this type occurs, stop teaching and immediately point out the problem and the potential for harm, warning that further incidents of this nature will not be tolerated. The prankster who initiated this problem also should stay after class.

TIP Keeping your thumbtacks in a drawer rather than on top of your desk and reminding students that their feet should be under their desk rather than in the aisle can help prevent some potentially painful pranks.

Occasionally something totally unexpected happens that is genuinely funny. It's the type of moment that is seen on shows that feature hilarious amateur video clips. A pen filling a student's mouth with ink, a window shade falling down when someone tries to lower it, or an unexpected pratfall certainly aren't high humor, but these events will send a class into hysterics. Take a moment to enjoy these unplanned and unintentional acts, laugh, and then get back to the lesson.

Making Silly Noises

The class is quietly working when suddenly a noise breaks the silence. It might be an animal sound, the smacking of lips, a fart imitation, or some other inappropriate sound. Tapping is a common noise, as is squeaking shoes when the floor is wet, whistling, humming, and scratching. Some truly amazing sound effects emanate from kids.

First, try saying something like, *"Please, let's not have any more noises; we have work to do."* That might solve the problem. However, some kids will risk a gentle reprimand and continue to disrupt class. Identifying the noisemaker could be tough because it's hard to identify the source of a sound. Because you would rather teach than spend your time rooting out the culprit, here's a couple of tactics that usually work and provide a deterrent to further disruptions.

Suppose you are about to begin your lesson when a rhythmic tapping captures everyone's attention. First, make a light remark such as, *"With a sense of rhythm like that, you definitely ought to consider joining the band. Unfortunately, this is language arts, so I need the tapping to stop."* This kind of comment usually does it. It also doesn't punish or single out the tapper, which is important because the tapper may not have even been aware he was doing it.

If the tapping starts again, stop teaching and then look in the direction of the sound and say, *"I need the tapping to stop immediately."* If the tapping begins again, say, *"If I hear the noise again, I will ask everyone in that group (indicating the approximate area where the sound is coming from) to stay after class until I find out who is making the noise."* That should end it because the tapper will receive negative peer response if he continues. The group will not want to stay after class because one kid wouldn't stop tapping.

> T I P   Remember to remain friendly and avoid raising your voice as you seek to end the repetitive noise. If you become agitated, the kids will see the noise bugs you, and more noisemakers may join in.

Here's a slightly different way of dealing with the same problem. When the noise occurs, calmly say, *"Let's just all close our eyes a moment and remember back when we were in second grade and kids*

Digital Watch Revenge

I have been known to incorporate a little revenge into my discipline. It isn't a good thing to do, but it can solve the problem. For example, when digital watches first came out in the late 1970s, many of them had alarms that played tunes. A kid in my class had one that played "The Yellow Rose of Texas," and almost every day, usually when I was trying to lead the class in a lecture or discussion, his watch would sing out. The kid always pretended to be surprised and claimed he didn't know how to operate his watch, but I could see he certainly enjoyed being in the spotlight. One day when it went off, I had him bring me his watch, saying that I would disarm it so it wouldn't go off during my class again. As soon as he handed me the watch, I quickly reset it to go off at 4 A.M. The next day he told me his watch had awakened him in the middle of the night. After that he apparently learned how to work his watch because I never heard its alarm again, and he never complained about losing sleep.

used to do noises like that all the time. It was a funny, little-kid thing to do. Of course, some of you still act like second graders even though you're now in eighth grade." That comment usually shuts up the noisemakers. It also sends a message to future would-be comedians that acting up might be an embarrassing thing to do in your class.

Talking

Kids never run out of things to say to each other. The fact that you are standing in front of the class trying to teach hardly deters them from carrying on with their conversations. Try these strategies to encourage them to be quiet:

- **Raise your voice and say something such as, "*I need you to be quiet.*"** This option works if a number of students have tuned you out and are unaware that you are teaching. This situation might occur if you come from the back of the room to the front and then attempt to get their attention. Do not continue to teach until all students are quiet. Just stand there and wait. Once they have seen you and have become quiet, begin speaking in a normal tone of voice. Speaking while they are talking indicates that it is all right to talk while you are teaching, and others will join in. Have a marker in your hand, and if the talking starts again, write the talker's name on the board.

- **Lower your voice.** When you have information that students must know, such as what page the assignment is on or where needed resources can be found, lower your voice and continue with the lesson. Those students who have been struggling to hear will become alarmed. Because they aren't able read your lips, these individuals will start making "sshhh" sounds and giving the talkers dirty looks. Invariably the din will subside, and you will be able to continue teaching in your normal voice.

- **Stop teaching and stand silently.** If the talking continues, say, "*I can't continue until everyone is quiet.*" Then stand quietly looking directly at those students who are disturbing the class. Even though you haven't made a threat about what will happen if they continue to talk, this action quiets the class almost every time. If a few students don't get the message, pick up a marker and write their names on the board.

- **Threaten to give homework.** Sometimes you find yourself constantly reminding your students to be quiet. Even writing names on the board doesn't stop the restlessness. In this case, let your class know that all this talking has consequences by saying, *"With all this talking and interrupting going on, we're just not making enough progress on this lesson. If we can't get it done in class, then it will have to be done as homework tonight. Let's try once more."* Peer pressure becomes a factor at this point as students start to shush the talkers. Note that this homework is not an extra assignment given as punishment; it is a natural consequence of the disruption. The day's planned work must be taken home because it could not be completed during the class period.

- **Mention staying after class.** This tactic is particularly effective when used near the end of the class period. Just say, *"Every time you talk, I'll be quiet. But we need to finish this lesson today, and I'm afraid you might have to stay after the bell rings in order to finish."* Invariably this declaration is followed by some frantic shushing noises, and then you have the quiet you need to teach.

- **Focus on one talker.** While looking directly at one student who is talking, lower your voice and speak to her. The rest of the class, being naturally curious, will stop talking to listen in on your conversation. Exactly what you say isn't all that important, although you may want to ask for the student's cooperation so that you can begin teaching again.

Blurting and Interrupting

Some students speak spontaneously, cutting you off in mid-sentence. They may be answering or asking questions about the lesson you're teaching, or they may be saying something that makes no sense at all.

In any event, their words come without invitation and disrupt whatever you were trying to do.

Almost every class has blurters and interrupters. These students may be so eager to contribute to the class that they impulsively speak their minds, or they may be vying for the role of the class clown. Either way, they must be controlled. In a room full of students, the only way you can maintain order is to have students raise their hands if they want to speak.

In some instances, classes resent a blurter's attempt to dominate discussions or question-and-answer sessions. More often the group is content to sit back and let one or two students do the talking and the thinking. In these situations, it becomes easy for the teacher to accept these impulsive answers, especially if the answers are correct or are good contributions. But if the class as a whole is to benefit from discussions, the teacher needs to stop the blurting.

The first time a student blurts out a comment or answer, accept his contribution, but remind him and the entire class that you only listen to those students who raise their hands. If the interruptions continue, put the interrupters' names on the board. Those students who chronically blurt out may have a hard time controlling themselves. Seating these students near where you lecture enables you to give them quick looks or hand signals as they are getting ready to interrupt. Consider meeting with such students privately to discuss this matter. During the meeting, compliment them on their willingness to contribute, but point out that they must raise their hand.

Acceptable Talking

When you are teaching a lesson or students are reciting, no one else should be talking. Likewise, when the class takes a test or needs to concentrate on an assignment, nothing less than silence is acceptable. However, being quiet is not natural for junior high students unless they are sleeping. It's important to recognize this fact and realize that sometimes it is acceptable for students to talk to each other during class.

Low-volume conversation is usually acceptable under these circumstances:

- When students enter class at the beginning of the period
- When students work together in groups on a lesson objective
- When materials are being passed out or collected
- When teachers are engaged in one-on-one conversation with a student and sharing information not essential for the rest of the class to hear

It used to bother me when students talked during class. My first reaction was to try to quiet the class back down. When I thought about it, however, I realized that although the noise bothered me, it was not hindering the teaching of the day's lesson. I discovered that my students were more able to listen quietly if I allowed occasional talking breaks.

Playing with Personal Items

Having a policy of not allowing students to bring personal belongings such as music players and electronic games into class not only eliminates potential distractions but also the possibility of these items being destroyed, damaged, or stolen. Make this policy clear to your classes.

If you see students playing with nonapproved items, such as toys, confiscate them. For first-time offenders, return the item at the end of the class period after warning them that if they bring more items to class, those items may spend a few weeks living in your desk drawer.

> TIP Never keep an item permanently. However, it's all right to play with confiscated toys during your conference period. Just make sure your students don't see you.

If you collect an item that, according to school policy, students aren't allowed to have because of safety concerns, such as chains, knives, or other potential weapons, turn these into the office. The principal's office should handle the discipline in these matters.

When School Supplies Become Toys

Students often transform everyday items such as pencils, pens, notebooks, and paper into playthings. A student unscrews a pen top and presses down the ballpoint ink stem, using the spring action to turn the stem into a missile with a range of three rows of desks. Wire spirals separated from notebooks become interesting necklaces and bad Slinkies. And each year students are fascinated by how a six-sided yellow pencil will roll slowly down a slanted desk. When students use school supplies for entertainment, mete out a reprimand or minor discipline for habitual offenders.

When Cell Phones Start Ringing

If a student's cell phone rings in class, have the student hand you the phone. Answer the phone by saying, *"This is Mr. Foley, can I help you?"*

If the caller is a parent or guardian, return the phone to the student and have her leave the room to finish the call. If the call is from a student and you are not in the middle of a "teaching moment," offer to relay a message to the student. This situation is often humorous if you can add a little wit to the occasion. After the call is finished, remind students that their cell phones are to be muted in class. School policy will spell out if and when cell phones can be used in class.

When a Student Damages Another Student's Property

If a student damages or destroys an item belonging to another student and that student had permission to have the item at school, then a solution has to be worked out. Wait until class is over and then get those involved together and hear what they have to say. Try to have them work out a solution. Don't let this situation degenerate into an argument. When they develop a plan, listen to it. If it seems fair, let

The Love Line

Around 1999 every classroom in my school building was supplied with a telephone. The phones were installed on the opposite side of the room from the teacher's desk, which made it hard for staff to monitor outgoing calls. Students saw this as an opportunity to gain access to the outside world. Some calls were legitimate, such as alerting parents about staying after school or begging parents to bring in forgotten clothing or homework. However, a clever student could use the phone for more devious reasons. To prevent this situation, I turned my room's phone into the "Love Line." Students could use my room phone as long as they finished the call by saying "I love you." Having to say those three words effectively shut off any calls except the most vital communications to Mom or Dad. As soon as someone got permission to make a call, the room would fall silent as we all listened to hear the caller profess his love for his parent.

them implement it. Check back later to ensure the proper action was taken.

In situations where the destruction was deliberate or resulted from negligence, the item needs to be replaced or repaired, and the guilty party must take responsibility to make it right. Again try to let the students who are involved decide the best course of action. Whether it involves monetary compensation, repair of the item, or replacement of the item, make sure that both parties are satisfied with the fairness of the arrangement. If the students cannot agree about the solution to the problem or if the guilty student does not take responsibility for his action, you may have to contact the guilty student's parent.

Writing on Desks and in Books

It's always satisfying to see students bent over their desks earnestly writing. At these times a teacher can't help but think that his or her talent as an educator has truly inspired the group. However, it becomes somewhat disheartening when, upon closer examination, the teacher discovers a student applying ink or pencil lead directly to the desk surface or onto the pages of a school textbook.

One way to deal with writing on desks and tables is to make sure every desk or table surface is clear at the beginning of the year and then walk through and personally inspect each surface at the end of each class period. That way, you immediately know when graffiti has been added and can identify the culprit. The desk writer then stays after class and, with a little cleanser, literally cleans up his act. A variation of this technique is to ask the class at the beginning of each hour if there any marks on the desk. At this time, the students look at the desk and bring attention to any marks that were obviously added by the student who sat there during the previous hour.

What's tough about this solution is that its success requires hourly vigilance. Personally I don't have the kind of discipline to be able to remember to check each desk every hour. Instead at the beginning of the year, I announce that writing on tables, desks, or other parts of the classroom is unacceptable, and if I catch students defacing a desk, disciplinary action will be forthcoming. Those students who are caught in the act spend time after class cleaning all the desks. If what they have written is an obscenity or otherwise a violation of school policy, then they are subject to disciplinary action in addition to cleanup work.

Catching those who deface school-issued texts or library books is tougher, and affixing guilt is nearly impossible if the book is not issued to a specific student. If caught in the act, a student should be required to remove all markings in that particular book. When students have assigned books, have the students check the texts on the first day and erase or blot out all markings. Then at the end of the year check the texts again. Those who abuse the book beyond natural wear-and-tear have to attempt to fix the damage or in extreme cases are assessed the value of the book.

Littering

Kids, by nature, are not good housekeepers. If you don't have a policy or plan to deal with trash, your room can look like a dump by the end of the day as paper wads, spiral notebook ravelings, and bits of miscellaneous litter cover the floor. Words of encouragement are rarely enough. Kids will not take the initiative of policing the area around their seats.

Some teachers don't dismiss their kids until all the trash is off the floor. To make this policy work, you must be vigilant and start with your first class of the day. Each hour must police its own trash. If you miss an hour and try to get the next class to clean up the floor, that group will protest that you are being unfair.

To be honest, I was never disciplined enough to remember to have each hour clean up before they went on to their next class. To keep the litter problem somewhat under control, I told my classes that if I saw students littering, they would have to pick up all the paper on the floor at the end of class. So then I kept an eye out, and it wasn't usually too long before I found someone dropping some trash on the floor. At that time, I would say, *"Tyler, I just saw you drop that paper wad on the floor. You'll be today's custodian and will pick all the paper off the floor after class."*

Inevitably it would occur to some that since Tyler would be picking up the paper, they might as well add some more trash to the floor. Anticipating this, I would add, *"Tyler will be the custodian unless I see someone else littering. If that happens, then that person will take over Tyler's job."*

Chewing Gum, Eating, and Drinking

To a student it may seem as though every classroom guideline begins with the word *Don't*. Chewing gum in class may be an exception. If a student can chew gum without distracting the class, it's not a problem. When a student's gum chewing draws attention, the gum is chucked in the wastebasket, and that student's gum chewing days are over. If you see a student sticking gum on the underside of a desk, then give that student the task of uprooting all other rubbery gum stalactites that are hanging beneath the other desks in the room.

Food and drink, however, are forbidden unless the student can produce a doctor's note saying he or she must have nourishment during class time. You must state this rule clearly, with the promise that if food or drink is consumed in the classroom, it will be confiscated, and the student will be staying for a few minutes after class. Pitch confiscated junk food into the wastebasket. If the food appears to be the student's lunch, return it as he or she leaves class after having stayed for a couple of extra minutes.

Being Tardy or Absent

If you don't have a plan for tardiness, it will become an every hour, every day problem. If the school has a tardy policy, just follow those guidelines. If it is left to your discretion, remember that consistency counts. Some teachers demand that all students must be in their seats when the bell rings; other teachers just want students in the room. Whatever plan you choose, communicate it clearly to your students and then stick with it. The logical consequence for being late to class is to be late leaving class. For chronic offenders, you may want to double the after class time or issue a detention slip.

To be totally consistent, you must be vigilant. Catching tardiness isn't always easy. At the moment the bell rings, you may be talking with students or other staff, disciplining a student, or helping students with homework. At these times, you may not see everyone who is arriving late.

Acknowledge that not every student who is tardy will be caught. Explain this apparent inconsistency to the class by referring to the example you gave earlier in the year when you outlined your discipline plan (see Chapter 1). In that scenario, you told your students that as automobile drivers if they choose to drive faster than the speed limit, they may get away with it. But if they are caught, they have no excuse and must pay the fine. The students understand this analogy. As long as you discipline most of the tardy students you see, your class will accept this policy.

Excuses for Tardiness

Student excuses offered for tardiness are usually pretty mundane. Occasionally some are quite creative, and a few, such as having a stuck locker or coming from a class that was dismissed late, may be legitimate.

In some cases, tardiness to the first class period of the day may not be the student's fault. Although sleeping in and loitering in the hallway too long are definitely a student's problem, the parent is sometimes at fault. Parents who frequently drop off their child at school late or require him to be at home to take care of younger siblings need to be contacted. Usually just asking students why they were late yields the reason for the absence. If the tardiness is obviously the parent's fault, inquire whether the family can make schedule adjustments to get the student to school on time. You or an administrator may need to follow up with the student's parents to make sure the situation is remedied.

Excessive Absences

To get an education, students need to be in school. Most absences occur when students inadvertently borrow from the community germ pool and need a day or two to rid themselves of the bug. Most school offices request that parents call in to report when their child will be absent and send notes explaining preplanned leaves. Each day the office secretaries telephone the homes of those students who are absent from school without an excuse. This process effectively catches students who are skipping school. Unfortunately, some parents call school to excuse their children and then keep them home to care for younger children or do other work.

Often when teachers are taking attendance, they ask whether anyone knows where the absent student is that day. This question prompts honest student responses detailing why the absent student isn't in class. If a student is caring for siblings or even playing hooky, someone in the class is likely to divulge that information. If you suspect that a student's absences are not legitimate, notify your school's administration.

Writing and Passing Notes

I suggest ignoring note writing if it is going on after class work is completed. However, if notes are being passed while you are teaching, you need to stop the distraction. Continue to teach and look directly at the current note writer. If she quickly puts the note away, I recommend letting the note writing pass the first time.

If the note writing starts up again, confiscate the note. The note writers will want to know what you're going to do with the note. Tell them that depends on how they behave the rest of the class period. When you do this, you are virtually guaranteed the note writers' total cooperation. Either return the note at the end of the class period or throw it away after class.

> T I P Never read a note aloud to the class. Although the content of most notes is fairly mundane, in some cases it may be embarrassing to the writer, her classmates, or you. Occasionally notes are profane or otherwise offensive. In any event, you never want to share this information with your entire class.

Occasionally, you might want to read a note when no students are present, especially if you have concerns about the student who wrote the note. The note may give you insights about her social or personal life that may help you work more effectively with her. Never share this information with anyone, unless the student has written about a serious personal problem. In this case, a referral to a school counselor may be appropriate.

Sleeping in Class

As you walk about the classroom spouting rhetorical magic, you are sure that everyone is enthralled with the day's lesson. Yet, when you look out over the sea of young faces, you see that one head is down on the desk; it's a sleeper. Your gut reaction is to walk over and scream in his ear or, as one of my former teachers used to do, drop a textbook onto the desk. The crash of the textbook hitting the desk inches from the sleeper's head rocketed that individual back to consciousness. Although that approach certainly has some appeal, it tends to disrupt the class, erasing from their minds all memory of what you were trying to teach.

More subtle strategies are effective in dealing with sleepers. When you note a student struggling to stay awake, try one of the following strategies:

- Direct a question to the student who is nodding off. Say her name first, hesitate a second, and then ask the question.
- Casually walk over to the sleeper and touch him on the shoulder.
- Stand near the sleeper's desk while you continue the lesson.

Don't criticize or discipline the student. The student's sleepiness may be caused by circumstances that are beyond his control, such as a crisis at home. In this case, embarrassing the student is not appropriate.

After class, ask the student what time she went to bed; often she will volunteer that she was up late watching television or surfing the Internet. Point out that this lifestyle is obviously not working for her and sleeping in your class is unacceptable. If the student's reason for drowsiness involves problems at home or personal anxieties interfering with sleep, consider referring the student to a counselor.

For those who chronically want to make the classroom their bedroom and whose lack of sleep comes from late-night recreation, stronger measures are needed. When they start to nod off, call them by name.

Drawing attention to them helps because sleeping in class is not considered cool among their peers. The fear of peer disapproval may motivate them to try harder to stay awake.

> **TIP** If several students are falling asleep in your class each day, you may need to reevaluate the content of your lessons and your teaching methods.

If a student falls asleep during the last minutes of class, let him sleep, but point out the sleeper to the rest of the class. When the class period ends, have the class tiptoe out so as not to wake the sleeper. I used to have one student reach up and cover the room intercom with a notebook to muffle the sound of the bell. Waking up in an empty classroom or finding themselves among students from a different class period seems to help tired students break their habit of sleeping in class. Other effective options for dealing with students who often try to sleep in class include changing their seats to be near the front of the room or having them stay a few minutes after class to make up for time spent in dreamland.

Teasing

If teasing happens while you're trying to teach, it's a disruption and needs to be dealt with in the manner that most disruptions are handled. In other words, direct the disruptors to stop the activity. If it persists, write their names on the board and keep them after class.

You will often find out about teasing when the victim comes to you seeking some relief from his tormentors. Have a one-on-one discussion with the victim, being sure to be out of earshot of the class. Mention that people who have low self-esteem and are hoping to get approval of peers at the victim's expense often do the teasing. Point out that teasing is often done to get a reaction out of people. Encourage the victim not to react and see whether the problem solves itself. Offer to give the victim a new seat farther away from his tormentor. Assure the victim that you will talk to the teaser.

As soon as possible, meet with the teaser apart from class and ask her to stop teasing. Sometimes the teaser may be unaware that her taunts bother the victim. Keep your tone friendly. Make it clear that if more complaints surface, disciplinary action will result. If the teasing is allowed to continue, other kids may join in, and a one-to-one teasing incident will quickly escalate to a group-against-one situation.

Teasing is similar to bullying; however, teasing is done without malice. Bullies, in contrast, prey upon the weak. Those who are being bullied don't enjoy it at all. For teasing, the teacher's approach is lighter; bullying requires a much harder line. (For techniques on dealing with bullying, see Chapter 6.) Nevertheless, the end goal is to make sure the teasing or bullying stops.

Some kids seek attention by being the victim. Somehow they get other kids to bother them so that they can receive your attention and sympathy. The more support you offer, the more frequently these individuals seek you out for solace from their tormentors. To prevent this behavior, find other ways to show interest in these kids. Having them help pass out papers or calling on them to recite in the classroom may somewhat alleviate their need for attention. Engaging them in conversation and showing an interest in them may help them get away from playing the role of the victim. If they continue to come to you with teasing complaints, do what is necessary to stop the teasing, but don't spend much time with the victim and offer only a token amount of sympathy.

Criticizing Your Teaching

We teachers are used to being the bosses of our classrooms. So when a student challenges us, wants to argue, or offers a suggestion, our initial reaction often is negative. After all, these students are just adolescents, and they don't know nearly as much as we do. Right? Maybe not.

When students question a statement you made, first examine their intent and determine exactly what they are asking. Are they sincerely questioning a point in the lesson, your viewpoint on an issue, or something else that you just said? The key word is sincerity.

If the student seems genuine, take the time to offer an explanation and perhaps ask the student to elaborate on his question. Listen carefully to the student and give consideration to his idea. Be open to the possibility that the student may be right and may have a better idea than yours. If he is right, compliment him and, if feasible, incorporate his suggestion into your lesson or classroom management plan or use it as a discussion item. Conceding a point to a student not only makes the student feel better about himself, but it also raises your status among your students as they realize you value their input.

If the student seems agitated or argumentative, his attitude and tone of voice will quickly indicate your course of action. Some students just like to argue and cause conflict. Other students think they are smarter than the rest of the class, including you, and feel the need to express that idea at every opportunity. The following sections suggest how you can handle negative comments from these students.

Arguing

If a student raises an issue that relates to what you are doing, address it. With comments on subject manner such as, "I think we were dumb to let the British surrender to us. We should have just wiped them out," focus on the historical issue. Follow these steps:

1. Listen to the question.

2. Ask for the student's reasoning.

3. Seek input from the class.

4. Add your ideas or explanation.

Use this same method of inquiry if the issue raised has to do with classroom procedure or school policy such as, "Why do we have to do book summaries?" or "Why can't we leave school during our lunch hour?"

> T I P You can turn the issue raised into a writing assignment such as a persuasive essay, a letter to the editor, or an appeal to the school board.

If the student is making a request that you can't honor, sympathize with the student and move on to your next activity. You might also suggest that the student take her concerns to the student government. If the student seems upset or wants to continue the dialogue, offer to meet with her after class or at another time.

Sometimes the student has an ulterior motive for asking a question:

- To distract you from the lesson
- To show off for the benefit of their classmates
- To pose a question that is irrelevant to what is going on in class

When this happens, try to deflect the issue with humor or offer to talk with the student about the issue after class. With these types of questions, speak softly and without emotion so the questioner does not succeed in disrupting the class or getting it off task. These students are hoping to provoke or upset you, so stay calm and deal with the matter without showing anxiety.

Occasionally you have a situation where the student just wants to argue. You have listened to him, given him an explanation, but still he circles back to his original statement and demands action. If he is repeating himself, getting emotional, or keeping the class from continuing, you must take action. Walk over to his desk and in a quiet, firm, but still friendly voice, tell him you understand his frustration, but there's nothing you can do now, and you have a lesson to teach.

Make it clear to him that you will be glad to continue talking about this issue and offer a time you can meet with him. However, at this point he must be quiet. If he continues to argue, pick up your marker, indicating that further talk will mean his name goes on the board. If he is especially disrespectful, you may have to assign detention or send him to the office.

Disrespecting the Class

Some students appear to be bursting with self-confidence and have no inhibitions about saying almost anything. If I tell the class that we are about to begin a poetry unit, these students say, "You know, Mr. Foley, poetry really sucks." Or they may inform me that poetry is a waste of time. These arrogant students will readily tell you how good they are and that they will get the highest grade on the upcoming test. Then quite likely they do just that. During class discussions when a student gives an incorrect answer, they are apt to respond by saying something such as, "That was a dumb answer. I can't believe you said that."

When an arrogant student makes an insensitive remark, stifle your impulse to get angry or counter with a cutting remark of your own. A good response is along the line of *"Comments like that are not appropriate,"* or, if the remark was directed toward you or your lesson, *"I understand you have a concern. If you would like to discuss it further, we can talk about it after class."* Do not let the inappropriate remark go without comment. If you do, the arrogant student will continue to address you and his classmates in this disrespectful manner. Additionally, others, seeing that you didn't address the issue, will come up with insensitive remarks of their own.

After class, explain to the student that you are open to sincere criticism, but in this case the remarks seemed designed more to get attention than to provide information. If the statement criticized a fellow student, then it probably shouldn't have been made. Furthermore, make it clear to the student that you will discipline him if there are more problems. Inform him that you won't call on him if you think he will make inappropriate comments. Giving him a seat in the back of the room might also help because it is harder for a student to disrupt class and easier for you to ignore a raised hand when a student sits in the back of the room.

Getting arrogant kids to cooperate can be tough because they have such an inflated perception of themselves that they feel no one can tell them what to do. If your talk sessions don't change their behavior, then you'll just have to respond to their comments with discipline.

Summary

Every year the faces change, but the problems remain the same. Teachers struggle with the same behavior issues whether their schools are in Tallahassee, Tempe, or Trenton. Use the strategies presented in this chapter to quickly end classroom misbehavior and return to teaching.

Keep these key points in mind:

- When dealing with pranks, silly noises, and other attention-getting behavior, remember to remain calm and act decisively. An overly dramatic reaction from you will just encourage more misbehavior.

- Make your expectations concerning student behavior clear. Be consistent with your discipline when those expectations are not met.

- When disruptions occur, handle them as quickly and calmly as you can and resume teaching immediately.

CHAPTER 6

Dealing with Disruption

With some classroom disruptions, it's clear how you should respond. As you learned in the last chapter, if students are playing with toys instead of paying attention, you confiscate the toys. If a student is late to class, he or she has to stay after class. But for many classroom disruptions, the solutions aren't so clear. How do you stop students who are bothering each other? What do you do with students who are chronic misbehavers? At what point should you ask for help? This chapter offers guidelines to help you handle even the most difficult classroom disruptions.

What to Do When You Don't Know What to Do

Even if you have been teaching forever and think you have strategies to deal with every conceivable disruption, some kid is bound to do something that leaves you dumbfounded. For example, Bill jumps up to touch the American flag and ends up tearing it off the wall. Jessica gets gum in her hair when she turns her head suddenly and snags the gum in Joe's hand as he heads to the wastebasket. Nick farts, and the whole back of the room starts gagging from the smell.

When you're teaching, an infinite number of things can happen, and when they do, you are judge and jury. Was it an accident or deliberate? Many times it's a gray area, but still you have to do something because these events can be like a chain reaction. If you allow them to pass unnoticed, you can bet more peculiar things will happen as kids test the waters to see whether the standards for acceptable behavior have sagged a bit.

So what do you do? First, quell the disturbance. Settle the class down. In the case of the fart, you may have to open the windows. Then look at the culprit who initiated the problem and sternly say, *"I'll see you after class."* By simply saying that, the instigator can only guess what fate awaits him, and you have bought some time to think through what the proper consequence should be.

Sometimes as you finish that class, you muse on the incident and come up with a logical consequence. At the end of the hour, listen to the student's version of the incident and then mete out the penalty. If it really was an accident, there may be no penalty.

On other occasions you're still in a quandary about what to do when the class period ends. So after everyone leaves, turn to the student and ask him to tell his version of the incident. You might have him clarify a point or add an observation before asking him, *"Something should be done here. How do you think I should handle this?"*

Ninety percent of the time the student will suggest a consequence that makes sense. Occasionally students will blurt out something that might not be appropriate for this incident but can come into play if further difficulties occur, such as, "Please don't call my dad," or "Don't give me a detention." Oftentimes students are the best ones to help you do the right thing when you're unsure of what to do.

How to Document Discipline

Do you document every time you ask a student to be quiet? Of course not. The day-to-day distractions are too numerous and, in most instances, are quickly handled with a stern look, a reprimand, or a name on the board. The goal of successful classroom management, after all, is to spend your time teaching rather than documenting discipline.

However, documenting discipline problems is appropriate in the following circumstances:

- When someone other than yourself, such as an administrator or counselor, will be asked to deal with the situation

- When a placement in a program for troubled youth may be considered

- When you want either a parent or administrator to recognize the extent of a behavior problem

A sudden explosive event such as a fight, insubordination, or violent outburst doesn't need documentation. The action is so outrageous that administrators are called immediately. The type of situation that needs documentation is where a student (or students), despite your best efforts of classroom management, continues to disrupt class. These problems are ongoing. I recommend that you contact a principal at the point that you begin making documentation, because if the student's problems continue, this principal will inevitably be receiving the documentation.

> TIP When you're stymied by a student's behavior, it's sometimes a good idea to share your frustration with a fellow teacher, counselor, or an administrator. They may offer a new strategy to try.

Unless you have an excellent memory, it's best to jot down notes as soon as possible. When the disruption occurs, first quell the disturbance, and then grab a sticky note, index card, or sheet of paper and write down the important details. Later you can type up a more coherent, better-worded synopsis of the incident. Keep this document where it's accessible so you can add to it as more problems occur.

In your documentation, you should

- Describe the disruptive behavior. Be specific. Don't just say, "He was bothering people," or "He kept fooling around."

- Give the dates and number of instances of the problem behavior.

- Explain how you responded to the incidents and what discipline strategies you used. Tell how the student reacted to this discipline.

- Indicate if and when parents were contacted and what their response was.

- Make a recommendation. You might suggest a parent/administrative conference, a suspension, a transfer to a different class period or teacher, or a test to see whether the student is emotionally impaired or needs special counseling.

Once you feel you have sufficient documentation, make a copy of your paperwork. Keeping a copy is important. If the problem escalates and you are reprimanded for being negligent, or if your building principal fails to support you, you will have a record of the problem that you can present to other administrators. However, keep in mind that these scenarios rarely occur. More typically when you show your building principal or assistant principal your notes, he will be receptive and will develop a plan with you that addresses the problem.

When Students Bother Other Students

You're up in front of the class teaching when a student tells you that someone is bothering him:

Ron: "Joe is bothering me."

Joe: "I wasn't doing anything."

Here's a way you might respond to this interruption:

"Joe, later I'm going to visit you at your seat and ask you to define what it means to not do anything."

This response gives Joe time to think. In addition, because you'll be talking quietly to Joe at his seat, he won't try to show off to the class when he gives his answer. Your discussion a few minutes later might sound like this:

Teacher: *"Well, what does it mean to not do anything?"*

Joe (whose answer may vary, but usually is something like this): "To not do anything means you're doing nothing."

Teacher: *"Should I ask Ron if he agrees with your definition?"*

At this point, Ron usually looks over at you and Joe, and it is apparent that he does have a differing opinion.

Joe (quickly speaks): "I was doing something."

Teacher: *"Ron, if it's okay with you, I'd like to know if Joe does anything in the future that bothers you. Is everything okay now?"*

You can't always take that much time to resolve this type of problem. However, you do need to respond to situations where kids are teasing or bothering each other. The first thing to do is to ascertain whether the antagonism is between two friends, two students of equal status, or a bully and a victim. Sometimes, when emotions run high and you must take action right away, you have to switch from being a teacher to being a peacemaker in order to resolve the conflict.

When Two Friends Disrupt Class

When one student complains that another is bothering her, consider that the students might just be trying to upset you and disrupt the lesson. This type of complaint is particularly suspicious if the students usually seem friendly with each other.

A good response to this situation is to say something like, *"If you two can't get along, perhaps I should separate you so that you both can focus on the lesson."* This statement works as a warning because the students know you won't hesitate to change their seats. The statement also brings the focus back to the lesson you are trying to teach. Under these circumstances, the students will usually cooperate because they don't want to be separated from their friends.

When Two Acquaintances Disrupt Class

Suppose a student complains that another student is bothering him. The students are not friends, but this conflict is not that of a bully and a victim either. In this situation, a seat change won't work because at least one of the pair probably would welcome a new seat away from the other. If the complaining student does not seem too upset, look at the other students and say something such as, *"If I hear about this again, I will need to work with you both to find a way for the complaints to stop."*

You should address both students because, on occasion, someone will falsely accuse another student in order to get him in trouble. Don't take disciplinary action unless you are sure what the problem is and who is causing the problem. Also, don't levy a penalty right away because sometimes the student is not aware that he is bothering someone until it is brought to his attention.

Your comment in this situation acknowledges that there may be a problem and also serves as a warning. The students now have the opportunity to change their behavior in order to prevent you from having to discipline them for disrupting the class.

If the bothering and complaints don't stop, ask both students to stay after class. Then talk to both students after class to try to understand what the problem is. Work together to settle the problem.

When a Bully Bothers a Victim

A bully is a student who picks on someone who is not able to defend himself. When this happens and you ask what the problem is, both parties, especially the bully, are likely to say there isn't a problem. As the teacher, you are unwilling to immediately stop class and deal with the situation, so you handle it in a similar manner to what you did when two acquaintances created a problem. However, whereas in that instance you said, *"If I hear about this again, I will need to work with you both,"* when bullying is suspected you say, *"If I hear about this again, we will deal with the problem."* The message is stronger and indicates that both parties may not be involved. This statement usually ends the problems for that class period.

After class, talk privately with the victim. Ask what happened and if things like that had happened before. You're trying to see whether this was an isolated incident or whether this person is being bullied on a regular basis. If the bullying goes on outside your class as well as in your class, you need to contact a counselor so she can work with the bully and the victim. If the problem only occurs in your class, try to find out what specifically is happening. Then ask the victim what might help improve the situation. Oftentimes moving the student's assigned seat away from the bully helps.

Then you need to have a private conversation with the bully. This conversation is a conference, not a confrontation. Don't get tough with him. Explain your concern, but try not to reveal that you have talked with the victim. Listen to the bully's version of events. Then ask the bully to tell you in his own words what bullying is. Having to define bullying may help him to see his own actions in a new light. Or he may just blow off the question and respond with, "I don't know."

> TIP Bullying often comes from feelings of insecurity. If you're able to establish a relationship with a bully, perhaps even help him redirect his energy to something like a school sports team, you may help boost his self-esteem.

In either case, you need to explain to him that every student needs to feel that he can attend school without being bothered. Then indicate that you will take whatever action necessary to make sure that students are not bothered. This warning may give the bully an out, in that he can say to his peers, "Mr. Foley's going to get me in trouble if I bother so-and-so again." The bully can now save face, and the victim is off the hook. At a later time, talk with the victim to be sure that, in fact, he is no longer being bullied.

> T I P Let the office know the status of a bullying situation. Also, you should document these situations so that a written record is available for clarification or corroboration if needed.

When you suspect bullying is going on, but the alleged victim claims he's not being bullied, you will be able to act only on what you see. If you see someone being bothered, treat the situation as a discipline problem and take action to stop the mistreatment of the victim. A seating change, time after class, a detention, a phone call to parents, or a referral to the office are all possible actions.

When the Conflict Escalates

The game changes when you have antagonism between two students. Instead of individuals acting out, you have adversarial situations, such as name-calling or even the threat of physical hostility. At this point, you must stop the lesson and deal with the situation in front of the class.

When students act out or begin to yell at each other, put a harder edge to your voice, something the class might not have heard before, in order to get their attention. Say that you will listen to each student's side of the story as long as the students follow these rules:

- No one speaks without raising his hand.

- No one interrupts a speaker.

- Physical violence or verbal abuse is not allowed. If any punches are thrown, the combatants will go to the office immediately.

Give equal time to each party and listen carefully. Offer advice or insights if appropriate. Your goal here is to help the students communicate and resolve their differences.

Sometimes this process leads to a spontaneous class discussion as the students work through a situation or explore an issue. Although your first priority is to teach the curriculum, when emotions run high and your classroom is in turmoil, it's okay to break away from the lesson and address the issue at hand. After the situation has been talked out and the class settles down, you should be able to return to teaching.

How to Remove Disruptors from the Classroom

Sometimes a student needs to leave the room. She's not fighting, getting belligerent, or creating the type of problem where a trip to the office seems to be needed, rather she is just incapable of behaving in your class on that day. Oftentimes she is part of a group that is so busy trying to entertain each other and the class that they are unable to pay attention to the lesson being taught. Not only that, she's interfering

Hallway Entertainment

I have stepped out of the classroom to check on a student that I sent to the hall just in time to see him propel himself off a locker with his feet and slide on his stomach across the hall. Another time, hearing animal noises, I found one of my students conversing in monkey language with another student stationed outside a classroom several doors down the hall. I've also seen students rolling marbles down the hall, shooting paper wads, or sliding pennies under doors.

Sometimes hallway exiles would still try to communicate with the people in the classroom by looking in the door window and mugging for their classmates. Once in a fit of desperation or perhaps inspiration, I taped a sheet of paper on the wooden part of the door with an arrow pointing to the narrow window where the student's face would appear. On the sheet I scribbled, "Look at me. I'm an idiot." When the student's face next appeared at the window, the effect was comical, and the class broke into laughter. The would-be class clown at first thought he was succeeding beyond his wildest dreams. In any event, that was the last time I had to worry about students in the hall peeking back into the classroom through the window.

with others' ability to attend to the day's lesson. Because this student has broken the basic classroom tenet of "Anything you do that interferes with my ability to teach or you or your classmates' ability to learn is a problem," you need to do something. In this situation, the student may need to leave the classroom.

In my experience, however, simply sending such a student into the hall or perhaps to a time-out room doesn't end the problem; it just moves it out of the classroom. Now the disruptive student can pretty much do what she wants. Students sent to the hall may wander about the school, visit the restroom, wave to kids in other classrooms, and in general have a wonderful time. Those who aren't bold enough to travel find plenty of fun things to do in the hall. For example, students who demonstrate no spark of creativity in your classroom suddenly transfer the contents of their pockets into toys and invent imaginative uses for them. Unmonitored time-out rooms soon pick up graffiti on desks, and trash is left on the floor.

After seeing the work of unsupervised kids left in the halls or time-out rooms, I decided to find them an environment that wasn't so stimulating. When I taught eighth grade, I worked in a school that housed grades six, seven, and eight. I had a good friend who taught sixth grade, and I arranged to send students to her room. In return, I offered to accept students from her. The arrangement worked wonderfully.

If either of us had a student who needed to be excluded from the classroom, we would give the student a pass, noting the exact time the student was excused. The student would leave her classroom and report to the other classroom. The teacher would check the student's pass to make sure the student hadn't taken a detour, and then ask her to sit in a vacant seat. The visiting student didn't receive a welcoming smile or greeting. Rather she was shown to a seat and then the receiving teacher continued working with the class. The students in the class were told not to interact in any way with the visitor, nor did the teacher pay any attention to her.

The students whom I sent found themselves being ignored in a classroom of strangers who were two years younger. I imagine that it felt somewhat embarrassing to be the big kid sitting with sixth graders. Students who were sent to my class were invariably meek and sat quietly. I imagine that it was somewhat intimidating to be a sixth grader sitting among a class of unfriendly eighth graders. Unless the student's pass said differently, I kept the student for the whole period and dismissed her with my class.

On one occasion, a student decided to use me as a sounding board to air a complaint about his referral. I listened. I then asked if perhaps I could set up a meeting so he could discuss his concern with his teacher, and I offered to be present if he liked. He fell silent and never got back to me about setting up a meeting.

At first, my fellow teacher and I weren't sure how this system of exchanging of students would work. However, we soon knew that we were on to something when our students would improve their behavior immediately when the possibility of visiting another classroom was mentioned.

We knew we would be defeating our purpose if we sent more than one student at a time to another classroom. In those instances where more than one student was involved, we lined up other teachers who would to be a part of our student exchange program. Between classes, we teachers would confer to make sure that the students we had sent had actually arrived. They invariably had.

Adding teachers to our exchange program wasn't hard to do. When other teachers discovered that we had effective places to send students other than the office, they were eager to participate. By not using the principal's office, we avoided the paperwork and follow-up meetings that often result from sending a student to the office. Substitute teachers also liked this system because it gave them a place to send students who were disrupting the class.

How to Handle Chronic Disruptors

Every once in a while you have a student whose mission in life seems to be to disrupt your class. When you're teaching or trying to get the class to work quietly, he's talking, whistling, tapping, moving about, dropping books, or poking his classmates. You begin to wish fervently that his family would move out of the district or that he would come down with the 24-day flu. However, typically this kid is vying for the school's perfect attendance award.

Although you feel that a strong dose of corporal punishment might curb his behavior problems, you understand this type of punishment is illegal. Instead, you have changed his seat, held him after class, created negative peer pressure, written detentions, and sent him to the office, but nothing significantly changes his behavior. He just doesn't care.

If he started fights, defied you, and dramatically disrupted class, he would be suspended or maybe tested to see whether he's emotionally impaired. (Those who are labeled emotionally impaired may be reassigned to self-contained classrooms.) However, he manages to just annoy you on a regular basis without raising enough commotion to get thrown out of class. If you ask him why he won't cooperate, he will likely tell you that he hates school and is just waiting to reach the age of 16 so he can quit.

Because you both are going to be seeing each other daily, you decide to adopt the effective tactic of building a friendship. Students tend to behave better and work harder for teachers they like. So you make an effort to get to know the student better by making contact with him between classes, at lunch, or during informal times in class. Try to find positive things to say to him. Be patient. He probably has had plenty of unhappy experiences with adults and may be suspicious when you offer the olive branch. Initially don't expect change in his behavior. He'll still head for the wrong seat, talk while you're talking, never have pencil and paper, and fail to do assignments.

During one of your conversations with this student, make an appeal to him by pointing out the things he does that are distracting and asking if he can help you out by changing his behavior. Sometimes students don't realize that what they are doing is disrupting class.

Much of the time changing a student's behavior is not that easy. In your one-on-one talks with the student, make your comments and questions more pointed. Let the student know that his behavior is causing problems for you and the entire class. Try one of the following suggestions or come up with your own way of making this point.

> *"Can you see how it might be difficult to pay attention to a teacher or get work done when someone is constantly making noise (or whatever the main problem is)?"*

> *"My job is to help students learn things so that they can succeed not only in this class but also in future classes and in the workplace. What you're doing is making it more difficult for me to do my job."*

> *"I have 30 students in this class, and I spend 5 to 10 minutes every day trying to get your cooperation. Don't you realize it's not fair to the others that I give so much attention to you?"*

End your talk with this question, *"Can you think of something that could be done or that I could do that would enable you to be less disruptive?"* Listen to his response. He may tell you something that will help. For example, he may tell you that someone is bothering him, that he can't see the board, or that he has trouble understanding the lesson. A student once told me he could do better if he sat by himself, a request I was more than happy to honor.

If he doesn't come up with something that might help you, explain to him that you are going to have to address his misbehavior. Point out that if you let him get away with misbehavior but discipline his classmates for the same kind of stuff, it's unfair to them.

Start by telling him that if he misbehaves, he will stay a couple minutes after class. If the problem continues after you have put his name on the board, you will issue him a detention form. If that doesn't work, inform him that he will be sent to the office. Expect him to say "Whatever" or "I don't care. It doesn't bother me." This comment probably will end the conversation. You have, however, given him a real chance to offer a solution, and he may now understand what you must do.

Starting the next time he is in class, put the plan into effect. I guarantee that initially he may just do his after-class penalty by pretending it doesn't bother him. But keep at it. There is no way that sitting in class can be preferable to walking the halls. Remember that if he refuses to stay or just leaves at the end of the class, he's earned a detention or a trip to the office.

In addition, step up your use of negative reinforcement. If making him stay after class and moving his seat away from his friends don't seem to faze him, begin to create negative peer response toward him by making statements such as the following:

> *"I hope you won't have homework tonight, but if Matt keeps disrupting class we may not get through the lesson."*

> *"Matt's antics have wasted some of our time, so we may not finish the lesson before the end of the hour. I'm going to close the door so that we won't be distracted by the students in the hall going to their next class while we stay to finish the lesson."*

Once the other students in the class see that Matt's behavior is causing them to get homework, leave class late, or miss out on free time or other privileges, they will resent Matt, who may change his behavior to avoid their disapproval.

During this time, continue to look for ways to have positive conversations with this student and compliment him if his work habits improve. Avoid confronting him, and never raise your voice with him. Be pleasant even as you discipline him.

In time, things may improve, or they may not. You will never succeed with every student. Expect to find some students in your classes who

Behavior Contracts: A Desperate Move or a Logical Solution?

Behavior contracts are sometimes referred to as positive behavior support plans, functional behavior assessment plans, behavior intervention plans, or even less imaginative labels. Most of the time in dealing with regular education students, you can skip the textbook chapter on behavior contracts. Although behavior contracts often help students overcome bad habits, implementing them is a time-consuming activity. However, if a student has elevated his ability to disrupt to an art form and has successfully thwarted every classroom management ploy, it may be contract time.

Typically behavior contracts initiate a plan wherein students are rewarded for doing, or in some cases not doing, specific actions. The best success comes when parents and students are involved in deciding what behaviors need to be changed and how the reward system will function. The contract invariably is written down and explains in detail what actions are needed to fulfill the contract and the frequency as well as the nature of the rewards. Many school districts have adopted a standard for behavior contracts so that all teachers follow the same procedures in creating them. In addition, the Internet offers an abundance of options for those needing ideas for behavior contracts.

Although I have dealt with some tough behavior problems, I never got to the point where I felt instituting a behavior contract was necessary. Periodically I had students, most generally ones who were diagnosed as emotionally impaired, who were on behavior programs that their special education teachers had developed for them. For these individuals, I would fill out daily progress reports and award points or rank their behavior on a numerical scale.

won't behave no matter what you try. However, most of the time persistence pays off, and even those who say they don't care may begin to cooperate.

How to Meet the Challenge of Students with ADHD

In the 1950s and 1960s, certain kids were called "hyper" or "hyperactive." A handful of these kids in a class would make a first-year teacher start wondering why she didn't go ahead and pursue that business degree. By the 1970s, science and psychological studies confirmed what harried teachers had been saying for years, namely, that these kids "weren't normal." Their condition was called ADD for attention deficit disorder and later renamed ADHD for attention deficit/hyperactivity disorder.

The behavior exhibited by kids with ADHD encompasses all the normal behaviors of kids but to the extreme. Whereas children are typically more enthusiastic, energetic, impulsive, and less attentive than adults, kids with ADHD kick this behavior up a notch. Their attention span can be so short, their activity level so high, and their self-control so poor that teachers and other adults find it nearly impossible to keep them focused long enough to finish tasks and handle normal routines. The behavior of a child with ADHD may be so severe that it impairs the child's development.

Roughly 10 percent of the student population is labeled ADHD or exhibits characteristics of that disorder. The following strategies are often helpful in dealing effectively with students who have ADHD:

- **Give them positive attention.** Although the AD in ADHD stands for attention deficit, what these students really want is attention. They want the teacher and their classmates to notice them. When they misbehave and the teacher corrects them or their peers react to their antics, they are receiving the attention they crave. Giving positive attention to a student with ADHD may prevent future misbehavior. Teachers who succeed with these students regularly give them compliments, smiles, and pats on the shoulder and find ways to engage them in conversation.

- **Supply immediate feedback.** Because a short attention span is a key part of their behavioral profile, students with ADHD need immediate feedback (both positive and negative) for their actions. Ignoring these students is a recipe for problems. If you don't pay attention to them, they will find a way to be noticed.

That's why teachers who understand ADHD find ways to interact with these students frequently in a positive way.

- **Tell them exactly what is acceptable behavior.** Define specifically what is expected of the students during class. Such expectations might include being in their seats, looking at you when you are talking, and raising their hands when they want to speak.

- **Offer tangible rewards and positive tasks.** Depending on the age of the students, giving gold stars, a piece of candy, or free time (but only a little bit) as a reward may keep them on task. Students with ADHD need to be active, so give them positive tasks to do. Washing the boards, picking up or passing out materials, running errands, and doing other classroom chores will channel their energy away from mischief.

- **Minimize distractions.** If you have seating options, go with rows of desks rather than sitting in groups or at tables. Assign them seats either close to your desk or where you spend your time giving instruction. Avoid sitting them where they can look out the window or into a hallway.

- **Keep your directions simple and clear.** When giving directions, only give one command at a time and don't address them until you have their attention. That means they are facing you and you have eye contact. If appropriate, ask them to repeat the direction. Expect to have to make the same request several times. Having instructions written on the board or posted in the room will minimize the number of times that you must repeat commands.

- **Provide simple and immediate consequences for misbehavior.** Reprimand these students using short, effective statements without raising your voice or getting emotional; don't lecture them about their misbehavior. Use the same classroom management strategies that you practice with your other students, such as minutes after class or seat changes. Be consistent.

> TIP   Students with ADHD typically misbehave to get attention, so try ignoring minor behavior problems. Encourage the other students to ignore the antics of the students with ADHD as well.

- **Get their cooperation.** Because students with ADHD are so active, their normal behavior can be distracting to teachers trying to maintain a classroom atmosphere conducive to education. Teachers may find themselves correcting these students virtually every minute of the class hour. This constant interaction can provoke hostility on both sides. Realizing this, teachers must work hard to build a friendship with these students. Taking an interest in them and finding opportunities to talk with them in the hall, lunchroom, or before or after class, can make a difference.

  When talk comes around to classroom behavior, point out that you realize that it is hard for the student with ADHD to stay focused on the lesson. Offer to use a signal such as eye contact, a touch on the shoulder, or a subtle gesture instead of a reprimand to indicate when he needs to pay attention or cease a distracting action.

- **Prepare them for special events.** Assemblies, field trips, guest speakers, and other out of the ordinary events often cause an increase in class disruptions. Students with ADHD especially have trouble adjusting to changes in routine. Talk to them, privately if possible, before the event and give them some guidelines on what to do and what not to do. Be as specific as possible in describing your expectations.

No matter how you may feel, be patient. Changing behavior patterns may seem like almost an impossible task, but take a deep breath and stay with it. Do your best to establish a good relationship with these kids, because they really want the approval of their teachers and their peers. Remember that ADHD is not an excuse for misbehaving or for poor academic performance. Work with these students to help them meet their obligations, be accepted by their classmates, and participate in all your class activities.

When a Student Refuses to Obey You

The problem is simple. You instruct a student to do something (or not to do something), and the student deliberately disobeys you. You cannot tolerate that type of behavior.

For example, Adam asked me to sign a pass so that he could leave the room to get a drink. I pointed out that my policy was to let students out of the classroom only if they had been doing work. Adam had been sitting at his desk doing nothing. I told Adam that if he would return to his seat and work for 10 minutes, I would let him go out for a drink. Adam said nothing, turned, and walked out of the room, returning about two minutes later.

What Adam did, leaving the room without permission, is not the issue. The problem is that he left the room when I told him he couldn't. So when he returned, I walked over to his desk and quietly pointed out that he had left without permission and would need to stay two minutes after class. He quietly said that he wasn't going to stay. I indicated that if that happened, he would be sent to the assistant principal's office. Because I wasn't actively teaching at that moment and the class was quietly working on a project, I returned to my desk and typed this short statement to the assistant principal:

> Mr. Jones,
>
> During class, students are allowed to use passes if they are doing class work. Those who don't work aren't given passes. Adam asked for a pass, and I pointed out that because he hadn't done any work, he couldn't leave. He abruptly left the room for two minutes. When he returned from getting a drink, I asked him to stay two minutes after class. He said he wouldn't, and he didn't.

I walked over to Adam's seat, showed him the note, and explained that if he stayed I would destroy the note. If he left, I told him, I would send the note to the office, and he would probably be put into in-school suspension. Adam chose to stay the two minutes.

In my dealings with Adam, I made sure to speak to him quietly, almost in a whisper, so not many students were aware what was happening. If I had made a big deal of this, Adam might have felt compelled to defy me to save face in front of his classmates.

> T I P Most students who defy teachers can be made to behave if the teacher refrains from being confrontational and allows the student to retain his or her dignity.

Although kids can anger or frustrate you, try not to let students see that their behavior bothers you. Talk with the students you keep after class. Try to get them to see why their behavior is a problem. Tell them you care about them and are concerned because you want them to succeed.

When a Student Threatens You

In a classroom situation where a student threatens you either by word or by action, above all try to remain outwardly calm. No doubt your heart is racing as you wonder what will happen next. Likely the student is emotional and may be yelling or even moving toward you. Here's what you can do:

1. Rather than face the student directly, turn slightly sideways to look less threatening.

2. Let the student have his say, and then in calm voice try to start a dialogue. Choose words that will not further inflame the student.

3. Ask another student to get help from the office or press the emergency help button if it is accessible. If possible, do this without the agitated student being aware of it.

4. If the student approaches, stand your ground, but be sure you are not cutting off his escape if he is about to bolt from the room.

5. Continue to talk to the student. Keep your voice strong, but do not address the combatant in a threatening manner. The longer you can stall the student, the more likely it is that help will arrive.

6. If the student attacks you and does not have a weapon, fight defensively to protect yourself.

When to Call for Backup

Skilled class managers strive to handle most student difficulties within the classroom. However, there are some occasions when a trip to the office is warranted. For example, fighting means an immediate visit to the office for both combatants. The teacher, however, can usually take care of high-spirited horseplay among friends.

If a student defies you, you may have to send her to the office. It depends on whether the verbal attack is directed at you or at what you asked. If she is aiming her frustration at you, an office trip is probably needed. If her outburst is about the subject, such as "I'm not going to do this stupid grammar," you may be able to settle her down by sympathizing with her or pointing out that the assignment may not be fun or easy, but everyone must at least give it a try.

If someone utters words or ideas that might be construed as racial slurs or sexual harassment, then you must inform the administration and send the student immediately to the office. These situations often get twisted when retold at home, and you could be the target of angry parents, lawyers, civil rights organizations, or groups looking for a reason to garner publicity. These problems can be minimized if you document the incident and involve the administration right away.

When a Referral to a Counselor Is Appropriate

When a student is frustrated by a situation outside the classroom (boyfriend/girlfriend thing, bad experience with peers or other staff, or family problems), she may walk into your class emotionally incapable of doing any work. On these rare occasions, you might let the student leave the room with a pass (or even a consoling friend) or stay in class and not do work as long as she doesn't disrupt the class. You also might encourage her to visit her favorite counselor.

Although it is not unusual for a student to have a bad day, a change in a student's demeanor that goes beyond a few days may be a sign that this student needs help. In many states, teachers are compelled to report any concerns they have about situations that may affect a student's physical or emotional health to counseling or mental health officials. Even if there is no legal obligation, teachers need to alert counselors whenever they suspect students are facing potentially harmful situations. For example, in reading over a student essay some years ago, I noted what appeared to be an account of a parent beating a child. I felt this couldn't be ignored, so I showed the paper to the school counselors. In another instance, a student's composition discussed his interest in committing suicide. I shared this piece with a school counselor as well.

Teachers should contact counselors if they feel any of the following situations pertain to their students:

- An obsession with death or suicidal thoughts
- Physical or sexual abuse
- Problems with siblings such as extreme harassment, intimidation, or abuse
- Unusually sexually active behavior
- High level of anxiety about home life, peer relationships, or the school environment

- A possible pregnancy
- Sudden change in behavior or noticeable mood swings
- Death or serious health problem of a close friend or family member
- Divorce or separation of parents
- Drug or alcohol abuse
- A home life that negatively affects a student's ability to function in school

This listing could easily be expanded because numerous factors can affect a student's mental health and well-being. Sometimes, although you can't pinpoint a cause, a student's behavior or appearance will change. If a normally gregarious student suddenly becomes withdrawn, sullen, or hostile, this change may be an indicator that the student should see a counselor. When a student appears in class sporting a radical hairstyle or starts wearing clothing quite different from her usual attire, this may be evidence that the student is dealing with issues where a counselor's expertise might be needed. Sometimes poor hygiene is a signal that a student is troubled.

> **TIP** Often it is best if the teacher first talks with the counselor before broaching the subject with the student. Then the counselor can develop her own plan for working with the student or do some background work on the student before making contact.

As a teacher you may feel that your relationship with a student may make you the most qualified to help. Although you certainly shouldn't back away from the opportunity to counsel a student, for serious matters it is best to get a counselor involved. Not only do counselors bring additional expertise to the situation, but they also provide some legal protection for the teacher.

Summary

Dealing with disruptions can be unnerving. But by using the guidelines in this chapter, you should feel calmer and better prepared to handle any difficulties that occur in your classroom. Keep these points in mind:

- In some cases, you may need to talk to students outside of class about misbehavior. Explain to them that you must be able to teach without disruption and ask them to help you solve the problem.

- Positive attention from classmates and you goes a long way toward preventing the behavior difficulties that are common with students who have ADHD.

- Don't try to deal with serious behavior problems all by yourself. Call on the school principals or school counselors when you need their help with certain students.

CHAPTER 7

Confronting Moral and Ethical Issues

Especially at the beginning of the year, students will question almost anything you ask them to do. For most of the issues regarding behavior, the explanation is simple and readily understood by everyone. I just refer to my all-purpose principle: *"If you make it so I can't teach effectively or you or other students can't learn effectively, then there is a problem."* However, some issues aren't easily explained by applying that principle.

In these times when society is redefining moral standards and ethical behavior, you may need to discuss such things as plagiarism, censorship, and prejudice in class. In addition, staff should expect to explain to students, even though they may not agree with them, why school rules on topics such as dress codes and the use of appropriate language need to be obeyed. Out of the classroom, teachers may struggle with issues of student privacy and wonder how much information they should share with other staff members. This chapter delves into these issues and offers some guidelines for dealing with these situations.

Facing the Truth About Lying

Lying is an issue that needs to be discussed with the entire class at the beginning of the school year. Start out by explaining how important it is to have integrity. Point out that most of us tend to believe that people are telling the truth, but when someone tells a lie, then that trust is broken and whatever that person says after that may be questioned. With kids, you usually have to point out that although they need to come forth with the absolute truth when attesting to whether they copied someone's homework or why they were late, the truth may be stretched a bit when a parent asks how his home-cooked meal tastes or a date asks how she looks.

Knowing why students tell lies helps when you are trying to deal with this problem. Here are just some of the reasons students tell lies:

- To avoid unpleasant situations
- To gain favor with others
- To cover their perceived weaknesses or mistakes
- To get out of activities that they feel incapable of performing
- To get attention

If you suspect a student is lying, be careful about confronting her. Your assumption may be wrong. Accusing a student of lying typically just provokes a denial. Unless you have definitive proof that she is not telling the truth, you have created a no-win situation.

When you do catch a student lying, the disciplinary action should be the logical consequence of the problem he was trying to avoid. If he lied about cutting in line, for example, send him to the end of the line. If he lied about finishing his homework completely, mark down the work accordingly.

The first time you find a student to be lying, review the highlights of the lecture mentioned in the first paragraph in this section. Then administer the appropriate discipline. Because lying often results from personal insecurities, you should make a special effort to develop a positive relationship with the student and work to build up the student's self-image. You can do this by focusing on the student's strengths and complimenting him on what he does well.

Confronting Cheating and Plagiarism

Certainly one of the most difficult situations that teachers deal with is cheating and plagiarism. Studies have shown that the majority of students attempt to cheat or plagiarize during their school years, and the problem is getting worse. With the Internet offering a mind-boggling amount of information, as well as Web sites designed specifically to offer ready-to-use term papers, research, and reports, students can easily avoid having to prepare original work for your class.

School administrations don't want you to take cheating or plagiarism lightly and have usually developed tough policies for dealing with dis-honesty. Students may lose eligibility for extra-curricular activities, may have to fail courses, or may be suspended from school.

At the beginning of the school year, acquaint every student with the school's policy. Make sure you carefully define exactly what cheating and plagiarism are and how they will be handled in your class. Provide each child with a written statement of the policy that includes examples of precisely what would be violations of the policy. Posting this information in the room further emphasizes your concern. Make it clear that there will be no warnings and no second chances.

As the students begin their first written assignment or take their first test, remind them of the policy. Informing classes ahead of time that those caught cheating will receive a zero on the assignment will dis-suade some from getting involved in the practice. Continuing to remind them periodically throughout the year, especially just before they take critical tests, is a good practice. Remember, adolescents have short attention spans and often appear to forget things almost imme-diately after hearing them.

Minimizing Cheating on Tests

Looking over and copying answers off other students' papers is the most common method of cheating during a test. You can remove temptation by spreading the desks out so that it's harder to see other test papers. If students sit at tables, place a folded divider between test takers. These dividers can be made of stiff cardboard. One teacher I know made his out of two pieces of plywood hinged together; these lasted throughout his teaching career.

Twins, meaning identical stupid or exactly worded answers on a test, are another sign of obvious cheating. To thwart this practice, make two different sets of tests and print each set on a different color of paper, so that you see at a glance who might be copying off a test paper. Although not foolproof, giving students colored cover sheets to use to cover their work should minimize the copying of answers.

Dealing with Dishonest Students

If you're going to accuse a student of cheating or plagiarizing, be absolutely sure you are right in your assumption and have evidence, in case you have to defend yourself to parents or the administration. Parents may protest school actions and bring lawsuits alleging either that their child was innocent or that the school dealt with the offense too harshly. For this reason, the teacher needs to be absolutely clear on the school's policy and absolutely sure he has evidence of cheating or plagiarism before penalizing a student. In the case of plagiarism, make a copy of the article, secure the book, or note the Web site where the material originated. In other words, make sure you have a hard copy or a way of producing the material that was plagiarized.

Hearsay and probable cause are not good enough reasons to punish a student. If you have strong suspicions but no hard evidence, either warn the students by telling them of your suspicions or watch them closely in the future. Warning students often acts as a deterrent and may keep them from attempting to cheat on future work.

When you catch students cheating, take time to talk with them. Explain your concern and point out why you must discipline them. Listen to them, be empathetic, and offer to help them so they won't have to be involved in this again, but don't let them off the hook. Follow up this talk with a talk with the students' parents to apprise them of the situation.

Don't ignore cheating or plagiarism; it won't go away. It's better that a student gets a zero on a paper or sacrifices part of his eligibility for his basketball season in junior high and learns a lesson about plagiarism at a younger age rather than forfeiting a college scholarship or losing out on sports as a junior or senior in high school.

Disagreeing with a School Rule

Schools tend to have a lot of rules, and as a teacher, you must enforce the rules even if you don't particularly agree with them. However, when students complain about school policies, you should try to avoid using "because it's a school rule" as your sole rationale. Instead, take time to discuss the issue so students can see some reasons for the school rule as well as understand that in our society it may be necessary to obey laws that don't seem relevant.

For example, the school where I taught had a rule prohibiting the carrying of backpacks to class. The students hated this rule and were quick to point out that carrying backpacks didn't disrupt class or distract students. I tended to agree with them, but realized that ignoring the backpacks would make it tougher for other teachers to enforce the rule.

So when the issue came up, I confided to my students that I didn't think bringing backpacks to class was a problem; however, I would not allow backpacks in my class. I noted how in some classes there was no place to store them and how in other classes, such as gym, theft was a problem. I also explained that after the shootings in Columbine High School some people were afraid backpacks could hide weapons or explosives. I went on to say that in our lives we would encounter laws that didn't seem fair or weren't applicable to our situation, yet we had to obey them. I also indicated that if they felt strongly enough they should take up this issue with an administrator or the student council.

Dealing with Dress Codes

Adolescents love to test limits, express their individuality, and rebel against authority by defying school regulations for dress, hairstyle, and jewelry. Those of us who rebelled against the dress code when we were students are usually horrified when we look back at our old yearbooks and realize that in our desire to be nonconforming and anti-establishment, we wound up looking comical and completely ridiculous.

The dress code issue persists, and teachers are expected to report or correct all violations of the school's dress code. Because most students who challenge the dress code are hoping to be noticed, teachers who publicly admonish them provide them with the attention they crave. On the other hand, no matter what teachers personally think, violations of school policy cannot be ignored because, unlike many policies where there is some gray area, the school handbook explicitly spells out the provisions of the dress code. The handbook describes what T-shirt logos are unacceptable and what accessories (typically chains and hats) are forbidden and states that hemlines can only be x number of inches above the knee (incidentally, let the vice principal do the measuring on that regulation).

The best approach to dealing with dress code violations is to talk quietly with the student, pointing out that a change is needed. He may need to turn a shirt inside out, remove jewelry, or wash off face paint. Try to catch the student as he enters the room during the passing of classes so you won't draw attention to him. Address the issue in a friendly, conversational tone rather than a confrontational manner. Your goal is to get the problem fixed without letting the rest of the class know.

If you notice the dress code violation after class has started, but no one is reacting to it, teach on through the hour and ask the student at the end of the hour to correct the situation between classes. If it involves removing a piece of clothing, send the student to the office. If the school has a dress code, administrators usually have a contingency plan to handle all types of violations.

If the students react to the dress code violation, calmly have the student leave the room to correct the problem. After making the needed adjustment, the student may then return to class. Don't mete out discipline unless the dress code violator initiates a disturbance. Sometimes the dress code violations may have occurred out of ignorance or forgetfulness. Often in this situation the student is relieved to make the clothing or makeup change because she doesn't want to be the center of attention for being different.

If the class wants to discuss the dress code, explain that the school population includes both the students and their parents and that clothing that most might find acceptable may offend some in the school population. The primary reason for dealing with dress code violations, especially in middle school and junior high school, is that unusual clothing or makeup causes a distraction. Teachers soon discover that whatever lesson is being taught is nowhere near as interesting as the kid with the green hair sitting in the classroom.

Censoring Class Materials

Every time a teacher shows a movie, assigns a class reading, or even brings a speaker to class, he must act as a censor. Teaching in public schools means being accountable to your students and their parents. If a teaching aid offends a student or parent, the teacher is usually held accountable, and the consequences may be severe.

Never show a movie that you haven't already prescreened. When you watch the movie, listen carefully for objectionable language and watch for violence or sexual activity that might be upsetting to your audience (or their parents). If you haven't read a certain book, make sure it comes from a recognized recommended reading list before you approve for use in a class assignment. If the speaker you brought to your class will be moving into controversial areas, talk with that person beforehand to ensure his talk will be acceptable to your audience and their parents.

> T I P To determine whether a certain book or movie might cause problems, try to imagine what is acceptable to your most conservative students and don't go beyond that level.

Students tend to be much more liberal than their parents and probably you. When they find out you vetoed the showing of certain movie or the reading of a particular book, they'll want to know why. The best answer you can give them is to point out that because attendance is mandatory in a public school, teachers have to try not to offend anyone, including students' parents. Although certain videos and books may have much educational value, there may be portions that some would find objectionable; therefore, these materials won't be used in class. Going to the movie theater or checking out a book from the library, on the other hand, is at the discretion of the viewer or reader; it is not mandatory. Readers and viewers on their own can be more liberal in selecting their entertainment. Although you are following school policy in dealing with these issues, at least you are offering your students a reasonable explanation for your actions, and this will likely gain you the respect of your students.

Curbing Inappropriate Language

Everybody's finally working; the small groups actually seem to be accomplishing something. Then you hear a word or phrase that you wish was "duck" or the recitation of the third person pronouns "she" and "it," but you and most of the students know it wasn't. A dozen pairs of eyes shift toward you. What are you going to do? You have several choices.

First, try to determine why the inappropriate word or phrase was spoken. Was it in anger? Directed to a certain individual or individuals? Expressing frustration? Responding to provocation or just spoken matter of factly?

If the word or phrase could be interpreted as a racial slur or sexual harassment, the student needs to be sent immediately to the principal

© JIST Works

or counseling office. Even though you may feel that you are able to handle the situation, these incidents can have legal ramifications, and trying to deal with them yourself would be mistake.

If the words aren't used to disparage someone and if their use seems to be accidental, you may be able to deal with the incident simply by pointing out that that this type of language is inappropriate for this classroom. Add that if it happens again, disciplinary action will be taken.

At other times you are sure it was said deliberately, perhaps to provoke you or to gain attention for the speaker. Again you need to make it clear to the class that such language is unacceptable. You then turn to the culprit who made the statement and say, *"I'll see you after class."* After class, ask the student to explain why he used this language. Listening to the explanation, try to decide whether this problem would recur. Then either dismiss the student with a warning that any further incidents of this nature would be dealt with severely, or if you feel that this might happen again, assign a time penalty of a few minutes after class. Point out to them that a repeat performance in your class will result in a detention as well as a call to the parent, explaining the situation and why disciplinary action was taken.

Occasionally you will hear the epithet but have no idea who uttered it. If it wasn't loud or directed at someone, stop class briefly saying that language like that will not be tolerated and then continue with the lesson or activity. If it was more overt, you may have to fall back on the plan offered in Chapter 4 in the section titled "Identifying the Unseen Disruptor."

Reacting When Students Accuse Their Classmates of Being Gay

Middle school and junior high students often use the term *gay* to indicate disapproval rather than sexual orientation. You might hear a student say, "Grammar is gay," or describe a certain TV show, food, or sport as gay. However, the term *gay* may be directed to people to mean that they are homosexual. This label can have serious implications, because the accusation of being gay to this age group suggests being different and being outside the group. And for junior high students, that's as bad as it gets.

Most junior high or middle school kids have little or no contact with homosexuals; their knowledge is often based on primitive stereotypes. The majority of schools do a poor job of helping their student populations understand and gain a mature perspective about homosexuality, so the students act out of ignorance. For example, if Jane is really mad at Ryan, she might say that he is gay. Usually the accuser does not really believe that the victim is a homosexual; it is just a way of getting back at a classmate or gaining attention from other classmates by bullying, because it is difficult to prove that one is not gay.

Nevertheless, the victim may be shunned by his peers. After all, in the eyes of junior high, to be friends or associate with a gay person means you might also be gay. And nothing the student can say will prove he or she isn't gay. If the word gets around, especially if others repeat the accusation, the victim may be ostracized. In some cases a student may quickly find himself without friends. Remember, these aren't highly educated or sophisticated people; they're just kids who aren't even old enough to drive.

Because this label can have such a devastating effect on a student's peer acceptance, teachers need to react instantly when they hear someone being taunted about being gay. If it appears that such a taunt is being used among friends and no one seems upset, it is sufficient to say something such as, *"That's not appropriate. I don't want to hear that again."* However, if the term is applied to someone in an unfriendly or nasty, teasing manner, just telling kids to knock it off may silence the disturbance, but it hasn't settled the problem.

To end the name-calling, say something such as, *"Wait a minute, how do you know this person is gay? To be sure, she would have had to tell you, or you would have to see something that would prove she is homosexual. I would be very uncomfortable making that accusation if I were you."* Follow this statement with a direct stare at the student for 10 full seconds of silence. If the student tries to laugh it off or deny his involvement, then this becomes a discipline issue beginning with a referral to a counselor or administrator.

The response I describe may seem politically incorrect and definitely moves into areas that are out of the realm of classical classroom management. Yet I actually saw students accuse a kid of being gay, and within days he went from a being a kid with a group of friends to having to sit by himself in the cafeteria. Several years later, he was still alone and virtually friendless. The teacher's goal here is to confront the situation immediately and put the accuser in an uncomfortable situation. This response seems to be the only thing that works. Afterward, the teacher needs to observe the accused student to see whether he is accepted by his peers in order to make sure that the problem was nipped in the bud.

In situations where the student body understands about homosexuality, the likelihood of students using the term as a slur is probably lessened. However, in student populations that are not enlightened, the fear and negative stereotypes associated with the word *gay* may be devastating to students accused of being homosexual.

Seeking and Sharing Information About Students

All new teachers will discover that seeking and sharing information about a student is one issue about which there will always be controversy. Some educators maintain that teachers must discover the nature of each student on their own. To learn about the student ahead of time could affect a teacher's treatment of that student.

However, virtually all staff believe that every kid starts with a clean slate the first day of school, so knowing something about a student shouldn't be a problem. Even though you may look at Jimmie sitting in the front row and remember his three siblings, all of them first-class hellions who terrorized you over the last several years, you're not going to hold that information against him. After all, teachers are professionals. They are not about to treat kids differently just because of what they've heard about them or who their family happens to be. If students are going to get different treatment, it will be because of what they do in class rather than what a teacher has learned about them.

A little background information may enable you to be more effective at classroom management. For example, knowing Jimmie has been a bully may help you zero in on a situation where some kids act as if they're being bullied. In this situation, you don't accuse Jimmie of being a bully; however, if you're looking at a group of students trying to figure where there's a problem, you might watch Jimmie more closely without reacting negatively to him in any way. He may have, in fact, matured beyond bullying, and the culprit may be someone else. The important thing is that you never treat Jimmie any differently based on his past history.

If you detect Jimmie bullying, then you address the problem. Treat it like a first offense, never indicating to him that you are aware that he has a history of being a bully. It would be totally unacceptable to make a statement as, *"I see that you're still bullying kids. I heard you had a problem with that last year."*

Asking Other Teachers for Information

If you have a student with problems and none of your classroom management plans has worked out, check with their previous teachers to see what worked for them. New teachers can especially benefit from ideas given by veteran staff who have had a few years to hone their classroom management skills. However, when getting information from staff about dealing with specific students, you need to consider the source. Although most staff know how to effectively deal with adolescents, not all are skilled in this area. You'll soon figure out which teachers are the pessimists and which teachers are overly critical of students. These folks won't be much help.

> **T I P** Remember that information learned about students from staff is just information. It's not a plan for action.

Prior knowledge should help you to provide a more positive experience for your students. For example, knowing ahead of time that a student is extremely shy, you wouldn't want to press as hard initially for that student to respond in class. If a student struggles with reading, selecting that student to read out loud might embarrass her. Finding out that an otherwise unmotivated student will apply himself to his studies in order to stay eligible for sports can be worthwhile information to possess as you try to get that student to be more productive.

Checking Student Records

Each student has a cumulative file showing his history since kindergarten. This file contains photos, report cards, testing data, discipline referrals, and a variety of other school-related information. These files are usually kept in the school office and are readily available to staff.

Elementary school teachers, who typically have 20 to 30 students in their classroom and deal with the same students for six or so hours a day, may find it helpful to consult the cumulative files. Secondary teachers, however, rarely review the files of every student. The job is too immense and is probably not necessary in most cases.

Student files are helpful resources when the teacher is dealing with a student who seems unable or unwilling to do classroom work. The file reveals whether the student has had a history of academic difficulties and how this problem has been dealt with in the past. The file may indicate that the student has been tested and perhaps is labeled as learning disabled, in which case the teacher may discover better ways to meet the student's needs.

Discussing Student Problems in the Teachers' Lounge

Although most of what is said in teachers' lounges has nothing to do with students, teaching, or schools, you will sometimes hear statements like the following:

"Mark is driving me crazy today. I'll bet he left his seat six times during the period."

"I finally lost patience with Shannon and gave her a detention!"

"Does anybody have any tricks for keeping Russell from blurting out in class?"

After spending several hours being the only adult in a roomful of adolescents, teachers often voice their frustrations when they finally get a chance to be with their peers.

To make statements like this in the presence of nonteachers or students is definitely unprofessional. However, in a teachers' lounge where only teachers are present, it is acceptable. Sometimes just talking about a situation helps. After all, the lunch period or conference hour break in the lounge is just a way station between classes. Talking about frustrations may relax staff so that they'll be more refreshed for the rest of their teaching day. Also, because teachers may be dealing with the same students, teachers who develop effective techniques for motivating or disciplining students can benefit everyone by sharing their knowledge.

> **TIP** Providing information about students can be vital. A recent divorce, a family tragedy, a health problem, or a traumatic event may profoundly affect a student when it occurs. Sharing this information with the student's teachers may help them to more effectively work with that student.

Teaching can be lonely. Even though you're surrounded by students all day, you see few adults. Except for the rare presence of a principal sitting in your room evaluating you or, if you're lucky enough, a teacher's aide helping you, no adult ever sees you teach. During times when you are struggling with classroom management or your kids can't seem to understand what you're trying to teach, it's easy to start doubting your qualifications as a teacher. Hearing others vent their frustrations in a teachers' lounge may help you discover that you're not the only one who is finding teaching to be a challenge.

Exchanges about students certainly aren't all negative. Teachers do have good things to say about their charges. You'll hear about great essays they've written, high test scores, sudden improvements in behavior, and sports achievements, as well as funny things they've said and done.

Summary

During the course of your teaching career, you will face many moral and ethical issues that fall outside the realm of basic classroom management techniques. This chapter explained how to handle some of the most common ones:

- Make it clear to your class that you will discipline any student that you catch lying, cheating, or plagiarizing.

- Adolescents like to challenge school rules, especially dress codes, in order to test limits and garner attention. You can often gain students' cooperation by discussing the rationale behind school rules.

- When students use inappropriate language in your class, take action to eliminate this behavior. You don't want to be known as a teacher who lets students swear in class. Slurs and name-calling in particular require immediate action.

- Gathering information about a student can help you be a better teacher to him, but you should judge his behavior based only on how he acts in your class.

Providing Incentives to Behave

Most strategies designed to get students to behave seem to depend on negative consequences. To keep them in line, you are supposed to keep them after class, change their seats, get their peers to disapprove of them, call their homes, send them to the office, or give them detention. However, you also can encourage students to do what you want by offering rewards.

Giving Positive Attention

Kids crave attention. Many classroom disruptions are simply attempts to be noticed. However, kids would just as soon be complimented as reprimanded. Too often the only time teachers remark about their work habits is when they're getting out of control. We teachers tell students to be quiet, to stay in their seats, and to get started on their work.

When things are going well and students are quietly reading, doing their work, or listening attentively, you may just silently accept this situation and enjoy the respite from having to correct misbehavior. Yet that's the time to build a little goodwill by commenting on how you appreciate your students' good study habits.

See if you can find the opportunity to use statements like these:

"It's really great to see everyone start their homework without having to be told."

"I appreciate that you're all working so quietly."

"Thanks for being so polite when we had the guest speaker yesterday."

"The bell just rang, and I see that everyone is in the right seat. That's great."

"It's sure easy to carry on a discussion when people raise their hands and don't interrupt others. I appreciate that."

"You're a great class; I enjoy being your teacher."

In addition to complimenting the class, you can give compliments and start friendly conversations with individual students to show that you appreciate the effort they're making to improve their behavior. Offering students opportunities to help out in class is another way to make them feel valued. In addition, students always like when you put in a good word for them with their parents.

Praise Individual Students

Compliments work wonders when given to individuals, especially those students who are usually on the receiving end of reprimands. If all they ever hear is bad news from you, they may think that you don't like them or that they aren't capable of doing anything right.

These students, however, have an image to keep up. They may want to impress their peers by being the bad guys or the class clowns. The best approach to take with these students is to compliment them quietly when their peers won't be aware. Consider variations on the following statements:

"You did a nice job today in class."

"Your work is improving. I like what you wrote today."

"Your cooperation in class has made it easier to teach. Thanks."

Your goal should be to say something positive to each student every day or so. If you can't find anything that you can praise, just initiate friendly conversations with students. Try greeting them at the door, complimenting them on what they're wearing, or commenting about a sport or activity they like. If you start the class on a positive note with them, they may be less likely to start trouble in class.

> T I P Avoid giving empty praise. If you praise students for the most mundane or dubious achievements, they may perceive you as insincere or phony.

I have found that it is also effective to make contact before class starts with kids who have been misbehaving. I might catch them as they walk in the door and say, *"I've got a tough lesson to teach today. Can you help me out? I know we've been battling lately. Let's see if we can keep your name off the board so that you can get to lunch on time."*

Ask Your Students for Help

In the traditional classroom hierarchy, teachers have all the knowledge, and students are the recipients of the teachers' wisdom. At the junior high level, this hierarchy of knowledge means that, except for pop culture, there isn't much that students know that teachers don't.

But all that has changed with the advent of the computer. Many teachers, especially those who finished their schooling before the Internet arrived, were somewhat intimidated when they found a computer installed on their teachers' desks. In short order, they were expected not only to do most school business including grades, attendance, and correspondence by computer, but also to start using it in their lessons.

When I started teaching in the 1970s, the most sophisticated piece of technology in my classroom was the pencil sharpener. However, I soon discovered that it would be my students who would lead me into the computer age. All I had to do was ask, *"Could someone help me with this?"* and a sea of hands went up. I never was lacking for technical support, and the students were delighted to help out their teacher.

Students aren't just eager to help you with your computer problems. They're ready to do almost anything for you. If you need signs made, papers passed out, notes taken to the office, or books straightened, call on students for assistance. Asking students for help provides you the opportunity to give some students attention and do a little more to build a relationship with them. Choosing students who are discipline problems to help you enables you to establish a positive contact with them. This time you're asking them to contribute instead of calling on them to behave.

Make a Positive Home Contact

Almost every time I called a parent or sent a letter home, the news wasn't good. The contact focused on their poor academic performance or misbehavior. I knew I should be taking time to call the parents of those students who were succeeding, the ones who got the *As* and had impeccable behavior, but by the time I had spent a couple hours calling the parents of problem children, I would be worn out. To be truthful, although I mailed or e-mailed progress reports to the parents of my best students, I didn't usually contact them personally.

There was, however, a group of students whose parents I made a greater effort to contact. Those were the parents of students who were doing better work or whose behavior was improving. Granted, it might only be to tell the parents that their child was getting a *D* instead of failing, but at least he was finally turning in some work. I would also call the home of a student who used to be a pain in the neck but was not acting out anymore. The parents on the receiving end of these calls were so relieved to finally hear some good news. In my experience, this type of phone call is a good way to gain home support and encourage continued good behavior from students.

Using a Class Reward System

One of my colleagues rewarded classes with stick-on bugs for good behavior. She would post the bugs on a chart in her room so that the students could see the class's progress. When a class accumulated enough bugs, it earned a reward.

If the class was seated and ready to work on time, it earned a bug. If the students were polite when a guest speaker or the principal was in the room, they might receive two bugs. If they cleaned up well after a science experiment, they might get another bug. They also could lose bugs for bad behavior. The system worked with her junior high kids who would do almost anything to secure a bug and even would try to stop those who were disrupting the class.

A jar of marbles is another variation of the reward system. If the class does well in a lesson or demonstrates good behavior, marbles are added to the jar. Marbles are removed when problems occur. A full jar guarantees a reward.

A class reward could be one of the following:

- A pizza or popcorn party
- A movie day
- A change in class location, either outside or somewhere else in the school
- Free time

Try asking students what they would like as a reward. Although some of their ideas are not practical or permissible, such as the ever-popular request to leave class or school early, they sometimes make reasonable requests that you can incorporate as rewards.

Allowing Free Time

Adolescents love free time. If I offered to give students a few minutes of free time in exchange for their cooperation so I could complete the day's lesson early, they would do their best. Frequent reminders along the line of, *"Gosh, I sure hope we can get done with a few minutes to spare,"* usually brought them right back on task if they started to stray. Although free time is an effective incentive, teachers need to use

Winning Their Minds by Feeding Their Faces

One common class reward is a pizza or popcorn party. However, classroom management can be daunting when you have a room full of kids celebrating with food. One can't help but recall what happened in the movie *Animal House* when John Belushi yelled, "Food fight!" and wonder if the same could happen in your classroom.

Some teachers keep a bag of candy in their desks and dole out sweet treats to those who keep their act together. One teacher I knew used to occasionally supply her entire class with lollipops on days when they were expected to work quietly. Her reasoning was that if their mouths were sucking on lollipops, they were less apt to talk.

Although popular with students, food is usually not the best choice for a reward. The increasing prevalence of food allergies and concerns about obesity in adolescents make it an unhealthy choice in the eyes of some parents and school districts. In addition, with a classroom full of kids eating pizza or popcorn, the logistics of cleanup may be a bit difficult.

it carefully so that it doesn't become its own classroom management problem.

Count Down to Free Time

The essay was due the next day, which meant my students were expected to be quiet and hard at work writing for nearly an hour. This was a lot to ask of junior high kids. So I wrote on the board, *"Five minutes of free time at the end of the hour."* I then told the students that every time I had to ask them to be quiet or a disruption occurred, I would subtract one minute of free time.

Ten minutes later, a couple of whispered conversations started. I walked to the board, crossed out *five* and wrote *four*. The conversations immediately stopped. A few minutes later another conversation started, and before I could react, I heard a "ssshhh," and the room grew quiet again. Because the incentive of free time was something everyone could enjoy, peer pressure came into play, and the class became an ally in my efforts to minimize disturbances.

The countdown system usually works well if it is used only occasionally. Typically the actual amount of free time ends up being two to three minutes. If the reward ends up being more than five minutes, free time is apt to degenerate into chaos. Unstructured time is best administered in small doses to students under the age of 16.

Prevent Free Time from Becoming Chaos

You and your junior high class have soldiered through 45 minutes of real education. You taught, and the students listened and responded appropriately. This is what teaching is supposed to be.

But now it's time to pay up. For 45 minutes of cooperation, you now owe them 5 minutes of free time, according to the deal you struck at the beginning of the hour. So you congratulate them on their good behavior, say, "Enjoy your free time," and walk back to your desk. You haven't taken 10 steps before chatter starts, several students get out of their seats, a paper wad arcs across the room, and someone yells, "Give that back!" Yes, free time has erupted on cue.

It doesn't have to be like this. Students can have free time without causing a ruckus. You just need to engineer and structure the free time a little. Consider these options:

- **Entertain them.** Share a joke or a funny story. If comedy isn't your thing, start a quick discussion about something your students are interested in, such as the best movie in town, what school rules they hate, the problems of cafeteria food, their favorite TV show, or the scariest thing they ever saw. Take a survey to find out their favorite sports, food, video games, or bands. These chats will help you better understand and enjoy your students.

- **Lay down some ground rules.** Before you start your free time, give your expectations. Remind students that there will be no shouting, throwing stuff, or touching each other or someone else's stuff. Then tell them that the third time you have to quiet the group down, free time is over. Also make it clear to the class that if this free time is chaotic, then the opportunity for future free time is in jeopardy.

- **Do an activity they like.** You students may have a particular educational game they enjoy playing or an issue they want to discuss. Hold this out as the reward they'll get for having a productive class period.
- **Provide games or reading material.** Have chess sets, books, or magazines available to keep students who have earned free time occupied and quiet.

Remember that when you're dealing with kids under the age of 16 who have unstructured free time, peace and tranquility are measured in seconds, not minutes, as you rediscover the true meaning of short attention span.

Bartering for Better Behavior

Sometimes a teacher has something a student wants. In these instances, a teacher can use that something to ensure that the student behaves well. That's the premise for the bartering technique. For example, you may have confiscated a note or toy that was distracting a student. When she asks for it back, tell her that if her behavior is acceptable for the rest of the period, she can pick it up after the class period ends or after school.

Any time a student asks for a favor, you have an opportunity to do a little bartering. For example, if the student wants to change seats to improve his social situation, you can offer him a deal. You might tell him that if he goes two weeks without getting his name on the board, you'll make the change. He can stay in his new seat as long as his behavior is good. Be sure to indicate that if he doesn't hold up his end of the deal, he will move back to his original seat and won't be given another chance to change seats. Note that you should do this deal-making in one-to-one situations rather than in front of the whole class.

Students may wonder if you're playing favorites when they learn you have been granting student requests. Therefore be sure you offer deal-making opportunities to all types of students. If done impartially, bartering is an effective means of improving student behavior.

> **T I P** Don't barter with students on a daily basis or even every week. If you do it frequently, every student will want to make a deal.

Summary

If you show your students that you appreciate their cooperation and good behavior through praise or other rewards, you may not have to spend so much of your class time doling out punishments. Keep these points in mind when you offer incentives to your class for good behavior:

- Most students thrive on positive attention, so you should be generous with compliments and offer students opportunities to assist you in class.

- Establishing a system to let classes earn rewards by not disrupting class is an effective way to control class behavior.

- Free time is a fine reward as long as you prevent it from degenerating into chaos.

- Occasionally you can trade a student a confiscated note or toy or a more desirable seat in return for cooperation in class.

PART II

Improving the Learning Environment

Successful teachers discover that part of the reason students behave is because they like the teacher, respect the teacher, and know the teacher genuinely cares about them. Students also behave if they are engaged and enjoy the lesson. That fact alone is a powerful incentive for teachers to make every effort to develop lesson plans that capture the interest of their students.

Being competent at classroom management is all about understanding the nature of adolescents and then making adjustments in the classroom environment to get them to want to do what you want them to do. The following chapters are full of ideas about adjustments you can make to your classroom systems and lesson presentations in order to motivate students to perform well in your class.

CHAPTER 9

Connecting with Your Students

The teacher is the focal point of the class and the greatest variable in whether a student succeeds. Few kids, especially those in elementary and junior high, enter their classes on a quest for knowledge. Their interest in the subject matter and their willingness to be attentive in class revolve around their feelings about their teacher. Students will behave better in class if they believe their teacher is a good person who respects them and cares about them. This chapter provides several strategies for making the most of your role as teacher and connecting with your students.

Appreciating the First Days of School

If ever there were a time when teaching seems easy, it's the first few days of the school year. The students show up on time, sit quietly in their seats, and look interested when you are talking. This honeymoon occurs almost every year and makes the beginning of a new school year a little easier. But don't think for a moment that the students are acting this way because they have heard of your reputation and expect them to dedicate themselves to their studies like monks for the rest of the school year. Instead, enjoy the honeymoon, teach your lesson, and keep friendly, but firm control of your classes.

> **TIP** The first few days of school are a good time to start building rapport with your students and establishing yourself in their eyes as a good person.

Even though the students sit meek as mice before you, take time to go over your discipline and academic policies. When the first bit of misbehavior occurs, react immediately by instituting whatever punishment you told them would happen. Typically that involves a name on the board or a seat change.

Becoming a Good Person in the Eyes of Your Students

In the late 1950s one of my junior high teachers announced, "This isn't a popularity contest. I'm the teacher, and you'll do what I say." He was right. He wasn't popular, and we students did what he said because to do otherwise would get us a boot to the seat of our pants or a slap across the face. But if his back was turned or he left the room, we would do anything we thought we could get away with. As far as our schoolwork went in that class, our own desire to get an *A* was the only reason any of us did well.

On the other hand, my junior high Spanish teacher, Mr. Smith, went out of his way to get to know all of the students in my class. For example, because he knew I loved to fish, he would talk with me about fishing. He spoke softly and conducted his class in a relaxed manner. We students liked him and felt he was our friend. We were attentive and didn't cause trouble in his class because we didn't want to disappoint him.

Mr. Smith had discipline rules that he explained were necessary so he could teach. If one of our peers misbehaved, the class viewed that student as the bad guy and viewed Mr. Smith as the good guy, even though he administered the discipline. How could we dislike or even hate a teacher who seemed to genuinely like us and had empathy for those he disciplined? He would tell them that he hated to levy the penalty (which was either detention or banishment to the hall), but if he let their bad behavior go without punishment, it was unfair to the rest of us. We students bought into Mr. Smith's logic and respected him even more.

As my experience with my teachers shows, teaching is a popularity contest in some respects because students behave because they like you. How do you get students to like you and still teach them what they need to know? You need to do four things:

1. Get to know your students.

2. Gain your students' respect.

3. Treat every student equally.

4. Show students that you care.

The following sections cover each of these topics.

Getting to Know Your Students

One way to get students to like you is to show an interest in them by getting to know them. If you are like most secondary teachers, you probably have five or six classes with anywhere from 125 to 180 students each semester, so you have your work cut out for you. As you put faces with names at the beginning of the year, you should also be trying to get to know each of your charges as individuals. Try these ideas:

- Greet students as they enter the classroom and when you see them in the halls. Even a simple hello shows them that you are friendly.

- Stop to talk and joke with your students in the hall or lunchroom and before, after, and during class. This contact helps you to see them as something other than names on a seating chart, and they get to know you in a different way. Comment about their clothes or talk with them about sports or whatever you feel is interesting to them.

- Open or close class by bringing up something nonacademic, such as television, the weather, current events, or the high school game last night. These conversations give you a chance to hear from and learn a bit about your students while demonstrating that you are a person whose interests extend well beyond being a teacher.

- To select a student for a classroom exercise, such as correcting daily work or homework, ask the class a question such as *"Who lives the farthest from school?" "Who was born the farthest from the school district?" "Who has the largest pet?"* or *"Who has run the farthest?"* Their answers tell you a little more about who is in your class.

- Let students know that they are welcome to stop in your classroom and talk either before or after school. When I taught, I was usually in my classroom a half hour before class started in the morning. I had visitors on most days, but they rarely asked for help with schoolwork. Mostly we just talked about whatever topic came up.

- On the first day of class, have your students write letters telling you about themselves. Not only will these letters help you to get to know your students, but they also will help you prepare to meet their parents at conference time.

- Invest some time with your students at their extracurricular activities by chaperoning dances and attending concerts and sporting events.

- Be friendly when you encounter a student outside of school. Because I lived in the town where I taught, I saw my students almost everywhere I went. When I encountered a student, I would greet him or her or maybe stop for a minute to exchange a few words.

Gaining Your Students' Respect

Gaining the respect of your students comes from treating them the way you would like to be treated. We all were once students and sat in classrooms for at least 17 years under the control of scores of teachers. We all can remember some excellent instructors as well as recall others who were truly awful. I resented those teachers who talked down to their students, speaking to them in a condescending manner. Instructors who had teacher's pets or showed favoritism to certain students did not get my respect either. I didn't mind teachers who were strict disciplinarians or tough graders as long as they were fair. When a teacher took the time to explain the rationale for a school policy or an action she was taking, my respect for that teacher grew.

This viewpoint probably came from my upbringing. My parents gave my brother and me the usual dos and don'ts to follow. Most of the rules seemed reasonable because it was readily apparent that following them would keep us from drowning or getting electrocuted, burned, hit by a car, or preyed upon by criminals. The reasons for some of their dictates seemed less obvious, such as being home by curfew, not going certain places, and keeping our rooms clean.

My brother and I were always allowed to question our parents' rules. They then would give us the rationale for why a decision was made. Questioning their decision and offering reasons for why it should be overturned was okay with them as long as we didn't get emotional. They would listen, seeming to welcome our input, and then occasionally would alter their dictate. More likely their original decision would remain unchanged. My brother and I felt like our parents respected us and valued our input when we sought a change in the rules. In contrast, I had a close friend whose dad also had a set of rules for his son. But if the kid asked why a decision was made, he was abruptly told, "Because I'm your father, that's why."

I decided that when I became a teacher, I would try to treat my students the way my parents treated me. However, taking that ideal from my home to the classroom proved more difficult than I imagined. For example, my parents just had my brother and me to question them; the classroom numbers were considerably higher. Further muddying the disciplinary waters was the fact that my students came from a gamut of backgrounds, had been raised with all types of behavioral expectations, and had been exposed to a variety of moral standards. I discovered that although getting all my students to buy into one set of classroom standards seemed at times to be as difficult as herding cats, it could be done.

Treating Every Student Equally

It's hard not to have favorites. Some students are just a lot more appealing than others. They enjoy talking with adults, may share the same interests, or perhaps are on a team coached by the teacher. You may find yourself paying more attention to these individuals than to others. However, if you do, other students will notice and will likely feel that favoritism is occurring. They are liable to perceive that injustices are happening when you discipline others but not your favorites.

In the classroom there can be no favorites. Make a conscious effort to get to know all students. You may not be able to have a conversation with everyone each day, but you should greet all of your students on a regular basis. Teachers tend to spend most of their time focusing on the extroverts, those who have the gift of gab. These students seek your attention by engaging you in conversation or through misbehavior that must be corrected. But beyond them are the quiet kids who aren't seeking your attention. These are the students whom teachers must make sure they connect with regularly.

Showing That You Care

Although students will often work harder on their academics or rein in some of their bad behaviors for teachers they like and respect, the results may be best of all when they know a teacher cares about them. If somehow students believe that their teacher's interest in them goes beyond whether they behave in class and master the curriculum, they may work hard to please the teacher.

Sometimes when I'm trying to encourage students to get their work in on time and do their best, I'll say something like this:

"I care about you. I want you to be able to live in a good house, to buy a snowmobile or jet-ski if you want, and to visit Disney World or go skiing in the Rockies. To do that, you're going to need at least a high school diploma and probably education beyond that. We're trying to teach you things that will help you pass eighth grade, be prepared for ninth grade, and eventually get that diploma. If I just let you goof off, it's not going to happen. You're not going to graduate. I'm available to help you in any way I can. I just need you to try."

> T I P   Don't be afraid to tell a student, "I care about you."

When you spend time getting to know the kids in your school by talking to them and listening to what's on their minds, they will begin to see that you're not just another adult, but someone who genuinely is interested in them. As you develop friendships with your students, they behave better and complete their assignments, because they don't want to disappoint you. The stereotype of the mean teacher has faded, and they now see you both as their teacher and their friend.

Remaining Calm, Cool, and Collected

Being animated in your teaching and perhaps infusing your lessons with a little drama is perfectly acceptable. After all, teaching is a little bit like the entertainment business. In both careers you are seeking to engage your audience and keep their attention. However, it's important to keep your emotions in check when you're dealing with class disruptions. Even if you're dealing with agitated students who are shouting at you, don't shout back. Speak with authority and remain calm as you deal with the issue.

> **TIP** Shouting may be warranted if there's a fight. A loud shout from you, especially if no one has heard you shout before, may be so startling that it alone may stop the fight. Also, science and shop teachers may need to shout if students are using equipment in an unsafe manner that could result in an injury or damage to equipment.

If the student is just upset and not maligning anyone, speak slowly and clearly, saying something like, *"I can see you're frustrated, but I need to get on with the lesson."* Then offer the student whichever option seems most practical: a pass to visit the counselor or an offer to talk to you after class. Make it clear to the student that she can't continue to have center stage.

If she appears to be visibly angry and still doesn't take your offer to leave class, point out that she must settle down immediately or you will have to take disciplinary action, such as time after class, a detention, or a visit to the principal's office. When students are upset, they are experiencing such a rush of emotion that they cannot always respond rationally. You must act directly and forcefully without losing control.

Teaching Your Worst Class

Students often ask, "What's your favorite class?" or "Are we your favorite class?" My answer is, *"I like all my classes,"* or facetiously I might say, *"You're my favorite class."*

Even though it may be hard to pick which class you like best, there's no doubt in your mind what your worst class is. Whether it's a scheduling quirk, fate, or bad karma, at least one of your classes inevitably has a disproportionate number of bad apples. Sometimes a few chronically misbehaving students keep the group in turmoil. In other cases, a group of very social individuals constantly disrupts the rest of the class. Whatever the case, such a class becomes a real test of a teacher's classroom management skills.

To succeed in this situation involves instituting a class management plan and then religiously following it. The names-on-the-board system coupled with a carefully planned seating chart usually works well as long as you are consistent in using the system. After explaining that those who interfere with your teaching or the learning process will have their names written on the board and will have to stay after class, pick up the marker and start writing. Students in these classes usually don't like having assigned seats, but the only way to break up talkative students is to put some space between them. If you are not getting the response you need in class, make phone calls home. Use detentions if needed, but try not to give them out often. The goal is for you to handle discipline issues on your own, not defer enforcement to the administration.

When faced with an unruly class, teaching the curriculum may be difficult at first. Because not much learning will take place until the kids are behaving, the focus initially will have to be on classroom management. Once the class figures out that there will be unpleasant consequences for misbehavior, they'll shape up, and you can start teaching academics.

Classroom management is never-ending with problem classes. You don't spend much time at your desk, instead you walk through the classroom, making sure students are on task. Although rarely do these classes become easy to manage, in time the students settle down, and you can relax a bit. However, you will probably always have a marker in hand to remind students that if they misbehave, their names will go on the board.

Peer pressure can work in these situations. What happens is that in your other, well-behaved classes, you will start to do more fun things, and the students in those classes will tell the students in the problem class about these good times. (You would be surprised at how much talk goes on in the lunchroom about what's happening in classes.)

In any event, the students in your problem class will want to get in on the fun. Point out that the reason that you haven't done fun things with these students isn't because you don't like them, but that you were afraid that if you loosened things up, there would be chaos. Students understand this logic. Tell the students that if they behave better, you will do fun things with this group. What you will invariably discover is that the chronic misbehaving students will be pressured by their peers to behave better. And when the behavior gets better, you can start doing some fun things in class.

Keeping Good Classes from Going Bad

Teachers soon realize that they have to clamp down on classes with problem students or an overabundance of youthful exuberance. However, the class that can become the biggest headache is the one you thought was your best class. At the beginning of the year, these students behaved themselves, were attentive, and did their work. So you loosened up a bit more with this group, kidded with them, and perhaps gave them some privileges. You relaxed discipline standards because you rarely had to keep anyone after class.

Gradually, however, you find yourself having to give this class more frequent reminders to be quiet and having to speak up because students continue to converse when you are talking. Realizing that you are letting these students get away with behaviors that aren't permitted in other classes, you begin to levy penalties on them, and they wonder why you suddenly are so mean.

What often works in this situation is to admit that you enjoy this class so much that you had relaxed your discipline standards, but now it is apparent that their behavior is interfering with your ability to teach. Admit that you are partly to blame for not being consistent, but you now must make changes so that they can get the full benefit of what you are teaching.

Having Students Evaluate Your Work

Having students give you feedback about your teaching is always enlightening. It can be too enlightening, because students at this age tend to be blunt. Yet often they are the only ones who scc you teach, and they're the only ones who can tell whether you are succeeding in educating them.

When you give a class the chance to do some evaluating, one or more of the following results is likely:

- You receive good feedback, the kind of information that will help you to be a more effective teacher.

- Students believe they have some effect on what goes on in class. This belief gives them a feeling that they are not totally powerless and results in a more positive outlook toward the teacher and the class.

- The students turn the evaluation into a gripe session, or they don't take the discussion seriously. The evaluation becomes an opportunity to goof around.

To increase the odds of a positive outcome, do not attempt an evaluation in a class where behavior problems are the norm. Select your best-behaved classes.

Evaluation seems to work best if it's done as a discussion, usually during the last minutes of a class period. Pick a time when the kids are in a good mood. You want this to be a positive experience. Preface the discussion with an opening statement something like the following:

> *"Students have taught me a lot about teaching. Some of the things that we're doing in class today are happening because my students gave me the idea. Now I can't even consider ideas along the lines of not assigning homework, giving free time every day, or letting you out of class early, but I am looking for ideas on how I can do a better job of teaching you. Are there things I'm doing that you would like to see changed? Are there things I ought to definitely keep doing?"*

Remind your classes that you would like to avoid comedy and just stick with ideas that are serious suggestions. Point out that what you are looking for is constructive criticism, which means you will probably have to define what constructive criticism is.

Listen with an open mind to their comments, asking follow-up questions to better understand their concerns. Answer them frankly and honestly. This is an excellent time to explain your rationale for why you select certain assignments or grade the way you do.

> **TIP** If you're brave and have a good sense of humor, invite students to do impressions of you. Not only is this usually entertaining, but by seeing others pretending to be you, you also can gain insights to mannerisms that you display and perhaps might want to change.

Summary

Every day teachers face a variety of choices in the way they deal with kids and how they do their teaching. In trying to decide how to act, I asked myself "If my child were in this class, what would I, as a parent, want the teacher to do?" Keeping that in mind usually helped me to make the right decision. Here are some other ideas to remember from this chapter:

- Teachers who are liked and respected by their students have fewer discipline problems in their classrooms. A good way to get to know students better is to talk to them about their lives outside the classroom.

- Establish discipline procedures at the beginning of the year and consistently maintain them throughout the rest of the year. Stay on top of your difficult classes and don't let your good classes slack off.

- Having students offer feedback on your teaching style and the curriculum can help you to become a better teacher.

CHAPTER 10

Answering the Hard Questions Every Teacher Is Asked

Some questions never go away. Each new assignment draws the same queries. Teachers can't dodge these questions, and answering them with a flippant, "I'm the teacher and that is how it's going to be," is easy to do but inadequate. Students need to know why the teacher sets certain standards and wants things done in a certain way. Students also want and deserve reasonable answers that explain the situation and offer a rationale for what they are expected to do in school. This chapter provides explanations that will satisfy the students' curiosity so that the question won't be asked again.

"How Many Words Does It Have to Be?"

By nature kids are minimalists. Every assignment is immediately analyzed, scrutinized, dissected, and reduced to the absolute minimum effort needed to secure an *A* or another grade that meets the student's needs (that is, their parents' expectations). Concepts such as intellectual curiosity and enjoying the process are not part of their educational plan.

Each year I optimistically thought that my new group of junior high language arts students would be different. So I led spirited class discussions about how exciting writing could be and how much fun it was to create your own stories. I read examples of past student work, helped them brainstorm for topics, and then told them to begin writing. Instantly a sea of hands was raised, and I knew what the question was going to be.

"How long does it have to be?" said the first student I called on.

"Oh, it doesn't matter. Just tell your story and don't worry about length," I responded, knowing that this answer would be about as effective as offering a starving animal a single French fry.

"No really, how long does it have to be?"

"All I need is for you to think up something that happened to you and tell about it." My voice was emphatic but my resolve was fading fast.

"How about I fell off my bike and broke my wrist, that's a story."

"All right, it must be at least 300 words."

"Can it be 299 words?"

"No, if you can write 299, you can write 300," I said evenly, thinking to myself what an idiot I must sound like.

What possible difference could one word mean, and why was 300 such a magic number? Couldn't a student write a magnificent narrative that was 150 words long? Of course he could. The truth was that I would give a well-written paper of any length an *A*. But after three decades in the classroom, I knew what would happen if I caved in on the word limit. If I said, "If it's good, it can be less than 300 words," I would set the downward spiral in motion. Instantly I would hear, "How much less can it be?"

Until you give students a firm, unchangeable word length, they will continue to try and whittle down the length of the assignment. Once you have established the exact word minimum, you'll hear their pencils, like gentle woodpeckers, tapping each word as it's counted. Tiny numbers between the lines of their rough drafts will mark their progress as they write their way to 300 words.

"Why Don't You Give Any Credit for Incomplete Work?"

Junior high students always want full credit for unfinished work, yet there are times when you must give no credit for unfinished work. When the final bell of the day rings, many students think that the end of the school day means the end of schoolwork as well. Even if you say the finished assignment is due the next day, work that isn't completed in class usually won't be finished.

On the day an assignment was due, I announced that I would accept only finished assignments. A student soon began the cross-examination by asking, "But I only have one question left to answer, can't I get some credit?" The only way I could make students understand my reasoning was to put it in terms of something they understood, namely sports. *"If a football player catches the ball on the goal line,"* I began, *"and breaks seven tackles as he makes a magnificent run 99 yards until he is tackled on the one-yard line, how many points does he get? Couldn't he get four or five points because he almost scored?"* Suddenly they understood why I gave no credit for unfinished work.

"Can I Write More?"

In my language arts class, I assigned book summaries where the absolute maximum word count was 150 words. Trying to cover the pertinent points of a novel's plot in 150 words or less was tough, so the students would plead to write more. "What if my summary is 151 words long? My book is really hard." However, if I weakened even a little, there was no stopping them. If 151 words were acceptable, for example, then is 155, 163, or 200 words acceptable as well?

When students asked, "Why can't the book summary be longer than 150 words?" my answer was simple. I said, "What happens if you walk 151 feet down a dock that is 150 feet long? You fall into the lake. That's why your book summary can be no longer than 150 words." I knew it was a stretch to compare lengths of book summaries to lengths of docks, but the explanation made perfect sense to junior high students, and they accepted the logic.

"Why Do You Mark Down for Late Work?"

Not all adolescents are obsessed with absolute standards, but most can't handle ambiguous requirements. Assign a book report, and immediately you'll hear, "How many pages does the book have to be?" Announce a due date, and you'll hear the following questions:

"Can I turn it in the next day?"

"Is the end of the day okay?"

"Can I turn it in after class?"

"What if I was absent?"

And so it goes. In time you'll learn to anticipate their questions and to have logical answers with examples and analogies ready. This way, even if your students don't agree with you, at least they will understand your reasoning. I think teachers owe students that much.

When I taught junior high, I made all my assignments due at the beginning of the hour. This deadline removed some time pressure by allowing students to finish work at home instead of having to finish it by the end of class. As soon as the bell rang at the beginning of class the next day, I collected the papers.

I told students to think of my deadlines like they would airplane departures. If you were catching the 9:15 to Detroit and you arrived at the gate at 9:16, you would miss the flight. This analogy made sense to them. (In light of recent news stories about the increasing incidence of airline flight delays, my deadline logic now looks flawed to me, but my example still sounds valid to students, who don't seem to follow the news.) I therefore imposed a penalty, a drop of one grade, if an assignment came in even a couple of minutes late. If I had no penalty, the homework would dribble in throughout the hour, and those frantically working to finish would pay no attention to what was being taught that day.

"Why Don't You Do Things the Way My Other Teacher Did?"

Comparisons to other teachers are inevitable, and most of the time the comparisons aren't favorable to you. If you're not getting compared to other teachers, you can assume your students like you or your way of teaching better. More likely you'll hear comments along the line of the following:

"We didn't have to do book reports last year."

"Mr. Jones let us do extra-credit work."

"Miss Smith said grammar was a waste of time."

"At my old school, you could have drinks in class."

Then there's the ambiguous statement, "You're not as nice as Mr. Johnson."

Your first impulse is to answer along the order of "That was last year. Now we're going to do it my way," or "Sorry, I'm not Mr. Johnson." Try to refrain from a hostile or indignant response that will alienate your class.

Instead, say something like, *"Let me think about that, and I'll get back to you. But for today I'd like to stay with the lesson plan."* If you can break away from your lesson for a moment, ask the students to get more specific with their concerns, and then try to respond so that they will see why you do what you do and how that is appropriate for them at this time. Oftentimes your answer will point out that now that they are in a higher grade, the curriculum is more challenging. When students question your methods or claim they like the way someone else taught better, address their concerns sincerely, and you will win their respect by showing them that you value their input.

Just by looking at the student who raises the issue, you can often determine whether the question is legitimate or just someone seeking to provide class entertainment. Answer a ridiculous question or one posed just to get your reaction with a humorous response or just by saying, *"Let's move on with the lesson. If you'd like to talk further about this, see me after class."*

Also keep in mind that you may not be getting the full story. Some of what you hear about other teachers or their methods may be fabrication, exaggeration, or just selective memory. No matter what is said, don't criticize the teacher. Your critical comments may find their way back to that person. Simply stating that you do things differently or that there is a variety of ways to teach a subject helps prevent strained faculty relations.

As a new teacher, you're apt to be questioned more frequently about the way you do things. In time you'll be able to anticipate the type of concerns students will raise and have a ready answer. However, you will find that some students make good points and that you might teach more effectively if you incorporated some of their ideas. Remember that they may have been in classes where things were done more effectively. There's no shame in borrowing teaching techniques if doing so will improve your performance. If you do change something as a result of student suggestions, thank them for their input. Knowing that you consider student ideas helps students to feel better about the class and you as their teacher.

"Why Do We Have to Learn This Subject?"

No matter how you answer this question, you are unlikely to see their eyes light up and see their lips mouth the words, "Oh, now I understand. It definitely is important for me to work hard in language arts because mastery of that course will be vital for success in my future career." Nevertheless, don't duck this question. Give students the best rationale you can for the viability of your course. Remember, whereas juniors and seniors may begin to sense the value of being an educated person, the masses in the lower grades are pretty much living in the present where the distant future is next month.

Most people need at least a basic understanding of math, reading, and writing in order to function in society, so it isn't hard to conjure up reasons why one needs to be competent in these courses. When giving reasons, you should use examples that are relevant to students' lives. With my language arts students, I noted how important it was to be able to write well enough so that a student could communicate his intent. For examples, I talked about writing a letter to the editor, a complaint about malfunctioning merchandise in which the student was seeking a refund, or a letter to a girlfriend or boyfriend to convey the student's true feelings about her or him.

Answering this question gets dicey when students question you about subjects such as algebra, social studies, literature, and science where it seems as if people can go through life and work in many careers without needing this background. For these subjects I point out how many people can't predict what careers they will finally enter. A quick survey and discussion about older siblings, adult friends, and parents will validate your premise. Therefore, because students can't know what the future holds, it would be foolish to not do their best in whatever appears on their course schedules.

Some students won't buy that logic, so go on to point out that one of the truths of life is that we sometimes find ourselves asked (or required) to do things we don't want to do. This will likely happen in their careers. Because they will be in this class until the end of the term whether they like it or not, they should put aside their prejudices and take a more positive attitude. Provide some examples about situations where people, after initially not enjoying an experience, found that it was better than they thought as they got more involved. Finish up by saying you will attempt to make the course interesting so that they won't be bored.

"Why Do We Have to Do Our Best on Standardized Tests If They Don't Affect Our Grades?"

By standardized tests, I don't mean the SAT and ACT that are the gatekeepers to getting into college, I am talking about the mandated state tests that are used to rank schools and determine funding. These tests are given during the school year, and by the time the results are known, the students have moved on to the next grade. So not only do the tests not affect their grades, they also might never find out how they did. No wonder students generate about as much enthusiasm for taking these tests as they would for receiving an enema (and enemas don't last for four to eight hours).

For teachers, however, the stakes are higher. Politicians, school administrators, and school boards paint a doom-and-gloom scenario for the district (and perhaps its teachers) if test scores are low.

When students ask why they should put forth their best effort on these tests, you should address the issue honestly. Begin by appealing to any sense of community pride or school spirit they might have by noting that when the scores are published in newspapers, people will be able to compare their school to others. This idea will connect with a few students in your class.

Then go on to point out what the politicians and education department of your state have projected as the consequences for poor performance. What you say depends on the state where your school is located. In this projection, show how poor test scores affect students directly. For example, reduced funding will affect those in your class, because funds will likely be trimmed from things such as athletic budgets and band or orchestra programs. Also, additional funds will be needed to create remedial academic courses for failing districts. This lack of funding will definitely lower the quality of a student's school experience.

Finally, if you feel your popularity with your students is high, make a personal appeal, noting that the scores reflect on your success in teaching that subject. Seeing good scores coming from your classes makes you feel great.

In the final analysis, no matter what you say some kids will do their best, and others will make a half-hearted effort. However, if you make a good case for taking the test seriously, some students who might otherwise shrug off the test will decide to try to make a good showing.

Summary

Just because you are the teacher, don't think that your students will blindly accept your way of doing things. Adolescents question everything. Keep the following points in mind so that you will be ready for any of the tough questions they throw at you:

- Adolescent minds only understand absolute standards. If you vacillate, they'll roll over you like a tidal wave. However, if you explain the situation in their terms, they'll accept it.

- Use analogies and examples that your students can relate to when you explain why you want students to do things a certain way.

- Even though students may not agree with you, they will respect you if you take the time to listen to their concerns and answer their questions honestly.

CHAPTER 11

Preparing Students to Work

Learning is an adolescent's most important job. Unfortunately, many adolescents arrive at school unprepared to work. They leave their books at home, goof off during class, and forget what homework they're supposed to do. The techniques in this chapter will help you get your students back on track and ready to learn.

Bringing School Materials to Class

Adolescents tend to tune out adults, so no matter how many times you remind them, they are still likely to forget things they need to bring to class. The strategies in the following sections will help you encourage your students to be more responsible and less forgetful.

 Students will come up with any excuse to leave class. For example, a paper cut needs a bandage from the nurse's office, and stuffy noses require tissue from the bathroom. To prevent these trips, keep a supply of essential items, such as adhesive bandages, safety pins, tissue, glue, and tape, in or on your desk.

Collecting Collateral

When students forget a pencil, paper, or other class necessity, loan them what they need, but collect collateral. The collateral can be a wallet, ID card, money, rings, or even a belt. If you just loan students pencils without collateral, they'll forget to return them, and you'll forget to ask for them. Make sure the collateral is worth more than the pencil and is worth reclaiming. Otherwise, you'll have a collection of inkless pens, used hall passes, and single sticks of gum.

Students can return the borrowed item for their collateral by staying a minute after class. If a student claims to have no collateral, ask him to put his name on the board. Tell him that you will rent him a pencil (or whatever else he needs) in exchange for a payment of three minutes to be served after class.

With chronic offenders, I gave them a pencil, but I tied a piece of monofilament fishing line on their spiral notebook and secured the other end to the pencil with duct tape. They now would have a pencil with them each day. Sure some of them broke the line (although I used line strong enough to land a salmon), but others were happy to not have to worry about where their pencil was when they arrived in class.

A colleague of mine deals with students who don't bring their materials by providing them with a folder with their name on it that contains pencil and paper. However, this folder never leaves the room so the student knows he always has the materials available when he comes to class.

Keeping a few spare textbooks on hand prevents students from leaving the room to go to their lockers to retrieve a forgotten book. By having a collection of novels and nonfiction books in the classroom, teachers can give those students who don't bring a book to class for a reading day something to read.

I know some of this advice sounds as though I'm suggesting that you should enable students and make it unnecessary for them to learn to come to class prepared. However, it seems to me that at this age some students, especially boys, just aren't responsible enough to remember. Many of these students make great strides toward being more responsible over the course of the year.

Hanging a Door Sign

Occasionally my classes had a reading day where students brought books and spent the hour reading. Because my classes had book summaries due about every six weeks, reading days helped me see whether my students were reading and to see what they were reading. The students enjoyed these days because it meant there were no assignments to do and no lecture to endure.

The challenge was getting all the students to bring the books they were reading to class. I tried reminding them daily, scrawling messages on the board, and having them write in their planners, but invariably when the reading day arrived, several students would face me with blank stares, mumbled queries of "Today's a reading day?" and no books. If I let the bookless students do homework, write notes, or work on the computer, the ones with books would complain. If I gave those without books an extra assignment, I would have more to do, and they knew they were doing meaningless busywork.

I tried peer pressure, decreeing that at least 85 percent of the students had to bring their books to class, or I would cancel the reading day. Of course if that threat failed and less than 85 percent of the class brought books, that class did the next day's lesson plan, which meant that class wound up a day ahead of my other classes.

Knowing that the students preferred a reading day to a regular day of English class, I recognized that coming to class without books wasn't an act of defiance, but simply was a case of forgetfulness. At this point, I came up with the idea of the hanging sign. I wrote "Reading Day Tomorrow" on a stiff piece of 8 x 11 manila file folder, and then used a length of masking tape to hang the sign in the doorway at forehead height.

As students entered the room, their heads would literally hit the sign. It was an instant sensation. Everybody read the sign, and most guys had to bat it. (I had to replace the masking tape with heavy-duty book repair tape.) The next day the sign said, "Reading Day Today," and nearly 100 percent of my classes came ready to read. The few who forgot their books were kidded about it by their peers. I learned that when I absolutely wanted my students to remember something, I dangled a sign in the doorway.

> **TIP** Everyone will read your reminders if you put the message on a piece of paper and tape it next to the wall clock in your room. Will they remember your note 10 minutes later? That I can't promise, but at least they can't say they weren't informed.

Listening to Instructions

Anyone who works with kids under the age of 16 knows nothing ever is heard the first time. A simple request to "Turn to page 421" is immediately answered with, "What page was that?" So you say again, "It's page 421." A minute later, a hand goes up, and someone says, "What is that page again?"

On the one hand, students must have the page number to be able to participate in the lesson, yet repeating the information only reinforces their habit of not listening. So how do you help students improve their listening skills so they will hear directions the first time? Before giving instructions, tell students that you will give lesson directions only once. When the inevitable question requesting a repeat of the directions comes, look at the student and say, *"We're starting on Page 421. I wish you had heard me the first time. Because this discussion now is taking away time that I could be teaching the lesson, you need to stay a minute after class."* Because students hate to miss out on passing time between classes, having to lose a portion of that time becomes an incentive to be a better listener.

Working in Class

Teachers can make sure the kids have the materials they need and are clear about the directions, but that is still no guarantee that they will get down to work. No, to get the project launched requires teacher vigilance. The following sections provide pointers for monitoring and assisting students while they are working on an assignment in class.

Keeping Students on Task

Immediately after formally starting the work process with the words, *"If there are no further questions, you can begin to work,"* scan the room to see if everyone has taken out paper, a writing instrument, and the proper textbook or handout. Then give them five minutes to work before walking through the class. While you move among the desks or beside the tables, look to see whether everyone has made reasonable progress in getting started. Are they on the right page? Doing the right exercise? For those with blank papers, inquire, *"Can I help you?"*

Most students begin working as soon as they are given an assignment. Others, however, need constant monitoring. Some students respond to assignments like dead car batteries; they waste time and accomplish little. Although electric cables would probably get a response with students as well as car batteries, you don't have to be that dramatic to get results. To jump-start these students, ask them, *"Would you rather work now or after the bell rings?"* This choice usually is enough of an incentive to get them on task. Note that this strategy should be used only with students who, although capable, are just choosing not to work.

As you sit at your desk while the students are working, look out over the class. At first glance, students may appear to be diligently applying themselves to the task. However, you should be suspicious of those students who are looking back at you. More than likely they are either trying to cover up a note they are writing, or they are ready to do something once you look away. Meet their gaze and smile, making a mental note to go to that desk first when you take your next walk between the desks. Periodically stroll through the room, going quickly to where you think students may be doing something other than the assignment.

Should You Walk Around the Class or Sit at Your Desk?

Walking around the room while students are working makes you more accessible to students who might be reluctant to venture up to your desk for help. They can receive quick assistance right at their desks without it being quite so conspicuous. When you move around, you also can glance at what the students are doing and assist those who are obviously struggling with the assignment.

The problem with moving about the room is what may be going on when your back is turned or you are bent over helping a student. Oftentimes, you can have better control of the class by sitting at your desk and letting students come to you one at a time. Try to arrange it so that when you are helping the student, you can still see most of the class.

Probably the best strategy is to do a little of both. Do some traveling around the class and spend some time at your desk. Let the nature of your class help you find the right balance of sitting and walking. Whatever you do, don't be predictable. If you follow a strict routine, your students will tailor their behavior to your known habits. For example, if you always leave your desk and then walk over to the nearest desks, the students in other parts of the room will pick up on this and feel comfortable doing other things, knowing that they can appear to be working on the assignment by the time you get to them.

Maintaining Quiet

Research shows that some individuals are quite productive even in an environment with many distractions. Unfortunately those who can listen to music, carry on a conversation, and overhear student gossip while working efficiently make up a distinct minority of the classroom population. Pin-drop quiet is needed when students must write creatively, read for comprehension, or do work that involves mental concentration.

If you want to receive quality student work, insist on silence during work times. This edict won't sit well with your students, who will point out that they can work well when people are talking.

One year I decided to test that theory. For several days, I allowed two of my classes to talk quietly while they completed a poetry assignment. Two other classes worked under an enforced silence policy. After three days, the quiet classes had accomplished twice as much work as the more social ones. From then on, when students began clamoring for a less restrictive environment, I cited the study I had done and then asked them to work quietly. However I wasn't opposed to letting classes who worked well have two or three minutes to talk at the end of the period.

Offering Help

Some teachers move constantly about the room offering help while students are working on an assignment. This may be necessary with some assignments where many need help. If the same questions are asked repeatedly, interrupt the class briefly saying something like, *"I notice a number of you are having trouble with this point. I'll take a minute now to go over it again."* This kind of interruption is probably more efficient than going from one student to another repeating the same thing.

When the same student impulsively responds to every assignment by saying plaintively, "I can't do it," you need to respond differently. In this situation, the problem may not be the student's inability to do the work but rather her need for attention. If the student manipulates a teacher into providing the answer or doing the work when the teacher offers assistance, the student doesn't learn anything and doesn't have to face the possibility of failing at a task. Furthermore, as a result of the teacher's eagerness to help, the student may begin to think that she is incapable of succeeding.

When a student says, "I can't do it," or "I don't know what to do," he may be overwhelmed by the task. To help him, start by rephrasing the question or breaking down the problem into smaller parts and asking him how to perform a basic task. What you are trying to do is to help him see that he already understands or knows how to provide part of the answer.

Once you have supplied some basic information, help the student to build on that and get closer to the answer. In this way he is working with you to solve the problem rather than the solution coming directly from you. This procedure helps students feel more confident in their abilities and effectively ends questions of "I can't do it" from those who are just lazy and are hoping you will provide the answer.

Remembering Assignments

It happens every time a teacher collects an assignment. At least one student will innocently look up and say, "It's due today? I didn't know that."

A new teacher who repeatedly had told the class about this assignment might wonder, "Am I dealing with amnesia, brainwashing, or the early onset of senility?" No, it's just another example of the mental screening process of adolescents. Compared with peer group gossip, music lyrics, and other vital pop culture information, schoolwork due dates don't rate much brain space in their heads. To penetrate their minds, teachers need to be assertive in the broadcasting of their assignments.

Using Handouts and Posters

Every day I taught five English classes, and each student was responsible for writing six book summaries a year. At the beginning of the year, I spent nearly an entire class period telling the students how to do the summaries, which book types were acceptable, how long the reports had to be, what the proper heading was, and when they were due. At the same time, I gave them handouts with all of this information. (I've included the book summary handouts in this chapter as examples.) That's all some of the students needed. Working from the handouts and the lecture, they made all the deadlines and handed in properly prepared work.

Book Summary Information

Due Dates

The following are the dates for hours 1, 2, and 3:

- October 1
- November 14
- January 8

- February 19
- April 10
- May 28

The following are the dates for hours 4 and 5:

- October 4
- November 19
- January 10

- February 21
- April 15
- May 30

Book summaries are due at the beginning of the hour! If you're one hour late, the summary drops one grade. If a book summary is one day late, it DROPS TWO GRADES. Two days late, IT DROPS THREE GRADES. However, even if the book summary is really late, turn it in for credit.

Heading

At the top of the paper, write the following information:

- Your name
- Your class hour
- The current date
- These words: Book Summary

On the first line of the paper, write the title of the book. On the second line of the paper, write the book author's name. On the third line, begin the summary.

Hint: Immediately begin your summary. Don't start your report with "This book is about," "In the book *Tom Sawyer,*" or "The book starts when…"

FOLLOW THESE RULES OR YOUR GRADE WILL DIE!

- All summaries are due at the beginning of the hour.

- All books must be at least 100 pages in length.

- The summary may not be more than 150 words in length or less than 100 words.

- All books must be at or above your reading level.

- Books about movies must be approved.

- Turn in your book when you hand in your summary.

- Use the proper heading.

- Tell the whole story. A summary covers the entire book.

- All books must be a complete story, not a collection of short stories.

The worst thing you can do is to be dishonest by reporting on a book that you did not read. **NEVER FAKE A BOOK SUMMARY! Only report on books that you read completely.** It is better to admit you didn't complete the assignment and turn in nothing than to fake a book summary. A faked book summary will be marked as equivalent to two failing grades.

Occasionally the class will have reading days, but only if 85 percent of the students bring their books to class. I encourage you to bring your book to class every day because the class often will have spare time to read. That way, you won't have to spend so much time reading during after school free time.

These are the best places to get books:

- The junior high library will allow you to keep a book beyond the due date if you are using it for a book summary.

- The public library has a great selection of books, but remember that you must turn your book in to me when your summary is due. This means you may get an overdue fine of five cents a day.

- Borrow a book from a friend or use a book from the room library.

- Purchase a book.

Some students, however, still didn't remember the directions or lost the book summary information sheet. As the due date approached, they would ask all kinds of questions, such as when the summaries were due, what the required length was, and what the format for the summary was.

I then reproduced the pertinent information on large posters, which I hung in the classroom. Even with these visual reminders, the students would forget to look at the posters, and some still asked questions. In those cases, I would just point at the poster. Not having to answer the same basic questions dozens of times in the year certainly made teaching more pleasant.

Having Students Repeat Information

To make the process of giving directions fun, have the entire class parrot directions back to you right after you say them. Or do a question-and-answer exercise in which the whole class answers questions about the directions you just gave. For example, you ask, *"When is this due?"* and they answer back in unison, "Wednesday." Make a game of it! Students love to echo instructions or shout back the answer. If nonteachers were to look in on your class when you're doing one of these exercises and see you and the students bantering back and forth, they may think all of you are crazy, but on a closer look they would see you and the students having fun. These techniques are not only fun, but they also are effective. After one of these little call-and-response sessions, students rarely fail to follow directions.

> TIP If you're tired of repeating information over and over, write the page numbers, due dates, and other important information on the board when you give directions. That way you only have to give the information once.

Helping Students to Use Their Planners

Giving homework assignments orally is an exercise in futility. Students look at you earnestly, nod their heads to signal their understanding, and return the next day with no memory of your instructions and no papers to hand in. To remedy this problem, school districts purchase planners, giving one to each student on the opening day of school.

These spiral bound notebooks have pages filled with sport schedules, school rules, basic math tables, lists of synonyms, hall passes, and other information deemed to be essential to the student. Planners also contain detailed daily calendars. Here teachers can send notes home to parents or request that parents initial completed homework. The parents also can ask teachers to give regular updates on a student's behavior or academic progress in the planners. The primary purpose of planners, however, is to do what adolescent brains are apparently incapable of doing, namely to carry information about homework assignments from school to home.

For teachers the first step is getting students to bring their planners to class. To do this, have students hold up their planners at the end of class when the bell rings. Those who are empty-handed have to stay seated for a half-minute while the others with planners leave.

To ensure homework assignments are recorded, just end the lesson by saying, *"Now write this in your planner."* Then be specific with instructions about the nature of the assignment and give the students time enough to write down the information.

Summary

Teachers need to apply their creativity as well as their classroom management skills to combat adolescent forgetfulness and inattention. Keep the following points in mind as you try to teach your students to be more responsible:

- Techniques such as collecting collateral and hanging signs are useful when you are trying to get students to remember to bring their materials to class.

- By walking around the classroom as students work on an assignment, you can find the students who need help and the students who need a little extra motivation to start working.

- Handouts, posters, call-and-response exercises, and planners are all good tools to use to help students to remember information about their assignments.

CHAPTER 12

Providing an Environment for Achievement

Motivating students to begin their assignments promptly, try to produce their best work, and then turn that work in on time poses a challenge for any teacher. Some students automatically complete assignments; others work to collect rewards, and a few comply just to avoid consequences. Teachers need to know what will motivate the unmotivated. This chapter describes classroom management strategies teachers can use to help students be productive in class and presents options for dealing with students who don't want to do their assignments.

Motivating Students to Do Their Best in Class

Students are in class to learn, but they all go about it a different way, particularly when it comes to completing work in class. A few students hardly put forth any effort at all. Others speed through the work, and some have difficulty finishing it. The following sections provide ideas about how to encourage students to work in class and how to manage a classroom of students who work at different rates.

Making Sure Uncollected Work Is Completed

When you require an assignment to be turned in, you easily can tell who is doing the work and who isn't. It's tougher when you assign work that your students keep with them or that isn't going to be graded or collected. They're tempted to not do this work or to rush through it without trying to do their best.

Each day as the students walked into my language arts class, there were two sentences on the board that they were to copy and then make grammatical corrections. Because these papers were corrected in class and wouldn't be collected nor graded, a few students weren't inclined to do the work, or else they would put little effort into it. However, it was important that they take this work seriously, because periodically I would pass out a sheet full of uncorrected sentences that would be graded and recorded as a test. The daily exercises were where the students learned the basic editing skills they needed to do well on the test.

To motivate students to put forth a better effort on the sentences, I told them that each day I would randomly select one student's paper to grade. If the sentences were totally correct, then the entire class wouldn't have to do the exercise the next day. If there were mistakes on the paper I selected, then the class would do the exercise the next day as usual. If I picked a student who had not finished the exercise or hadn't even attempted to do it, then I would give that student a sheet with 10 more sentences to do for homework. If the student did not turn in the sentences by the beginning of the next day's class, he would receive a detention.

What this process did was create dual expectations. On the one hand, the students did the work so they wouldn't have to do the homework penalty of correcting 10 extra sentences. On the other hand, they wanted to do their best to write the sentences correctly in order to get peer approval.

When I found a paper that had no mistakes and announced that the class wouldn't have to do the exercise the next day, the class usually clapped and cheered. This feedback always made the authors of the perfect sentences feel pretty good. The ones who did well on this exercise often were the quiet, studious class members who didn't get much recognition, so they must have felt good to suddenly be the heroes of the moment.

Helping Students Who Can't Complete Work on Time

In junior high and middle school, realistic due dates are set so that the majority of students will make the deadline. However, students who don't effectively use the work periods during class still must meet the same deadlines as the rest of the class and suffer the consequences if they miss the deadline, which usually means a lower grade given to the work when and if it is finally completed.

During work periods, you should move about the classroom, checking to make sure students are making progress and helping those who are struggling with the assignment. When students encounter difficulties, many of them just stop working and don't seek help.

For students with learning disabilities, you may need to adjust deadlines or the requirements of the assignment. These students may be part of special needs programs or have support personnel who can help them. ADHD students also may get some special consideration, such as an extended deadline or access to a less-distracting working environment, such as home or a conference room.

Occupying Students Who Finish Their Work Early

Ideally due dates are established so that every student can easily complete the work on time. However, waiting until every student can complete the work means most students will have time on their hands, and the best students may find themselves getting work done in less than half the time of their classmates. Students who finish their work early become one of those good news/bad news situations. The good news is that the work is turned in. The bad news is that the student now has nothing to do.

When students turn work in early, quickly look over the assignments to see whether they meet the criteria of finished work. Frequently students rush to turn in work and either fail to follow directions or put forth a substandard effort. Including a checklist or writing directions on the board can help students to be more careful with their work.

If the assignments are incomplete, return them to the students and ask if they have any ideas how their work can be improved. If they seem perplexed, point out the problem areas and ask whether they can rework them. Avoid telling students what they must do, but instead have them examine certain parts and ask them if they can make improvements. If you make specific corrections, students will rely on you to be their proofreader/editor. They will start visiting your desk regularly seeking assistance as they discover that they won't have to do much if you keep doing their work for them.

If assignments turned in early seem complete and adequate, then you need a plan to keep the students occupied so they don't disturb the rest of the class. To keep these students busy, you can let them

- Work on long-range assignments, such as book reports or term projects
- Read a book from the class library
- Do homework from other classes
- Work on computers, as long as they don't visit inappropriate Web sites
- Play chess or a board game quietly

As long as they're quiet, they can even write notes or doodle, although such activities are not particularly productive. However, playing computer games, which is typically a violation of school policy, is not acceptable.

Giving Students More Time to Finish Work in Class

As mentioned before, the best time to collect an assignment is at the beginning of the hour. However, with tests, writing projects, or other work that is not appropriate to send home, you may need to collect work at the end of the class period. In these situations, there will be students who do not finish and need more time.

Unless the assignment is a timed one, such as a standardized test, try to allow the students to finish. Typically those that need more time are often your best students who are meticulous and thorough with their work. When the bell rings and the class leaves, allow these students to either remain in your room or go into the hall after the bell rings starting the next class. Be sure to notify the teacher of the student's next class that the student is finishing work with you.

Handling Homework

Getting students to complete homework and turn it in on time is a challenge for every teacher. The strategies in this section can help you ensure that student work is complete, establish deadlines for students, and help students finish long-range projects.

Using Assignment Handouts

If homework and in-class assignments are not explicitly explained in a textbook, pass out handouts containing all the pertinent information so students won't have to keep coming up to your desk asking for clarification. As much as possible the handouts should be self-explanatory so that if they were sent home to a student who was not in school, she could complete the assignment. Assignment handouts, therefore, should contain the following information:

- A short definition of the assignment with an example, if possible
- If a textbook is to be used as a resource, page numbers where students can find pertinent information

- A clear explanation of what features must be a part of the assignment that is to be turned in

- The assignment due date written in large bold print

A checklist is a helpful format for an assignment handout. The checklist format not only helps the student to complete all assignment requirements, but also helps the teacher to more effectively correct student work. After passing out the checklist, take a few minutes to thoroughly go over it so that students know what they must do to successfully finish the assignment.

Because adolescents are, by nature, somewhat distracted, forgetful, and disorganized, a checklist helps them at least remember the requirements of an assignment. As students accomplish each part of the assignment, they check it off the list. When all blanks are checked off, the assignment is completed and ready to turn in. When students turn in assignment packets, the checklist is the top sheet.

For the teacher faced with stacks of essays to correct, the checklist provides a quick way to highlight strengths and weaknesses of the students' work, as you can see in the "Essay Checklist" included in this chapter. Rather than write, "This paper needs a topic sentence," the teacher merely checks or highlights the part of the checklist that deals with topic sentences.

Setting a Due Date

Determining the due date of an assignment involves factoring in the complexity and difficulty of the assignment with the capabilities of your students. For a first-year teacher, setting a due date is guesswork, but if you are working from a carefully constructed lesson plan, you may be able to anticipate how long most students need to complete the work. However, after you have done the lesson once, you will know. Just be sure and write this information into the lesson so you'll get it right the second year.

Essay Checklist

Every student must complete this checklist and turn it in as part of his or her essay.

Due Date: 04/15/XX

Turn In

☐ Checklist

☐ Final Draft (comes next after checklist)

☐ Rough Draft

☐ Think Sheet (questions and answers about essay topic)

Checklist for Final Draft

☐ Proper heading (name, hour, date, type of essay)

☐ Introduction (catches reader's attention, defines topic, tells what you are going to do)

☐ Body paragraphs (at least three paragraphs developing three ideas relating to topic)

☐ Conclusion (summarizes essay and emphasizes key points)

☐ Lines skipped or double spaced

☐ **At least 200 words in length**

☐ At least seven correctly used and <u>underlined</u> glue words

☐ No spelling errors, fragments, run-ons, or improper use of capital letters

Post every important assignment due date in the room. Have a special place for these notices. While pointing to the written notice, verbally remind students of the assignment. Don't forget to ask the question, *"Does anyone have any questions about this assignment? Please ask me now because I expect to receive this work totally completed on such and such a date."*

> **T I P** If the students have planners, have them take out their planners and write down the information about the assignment while you are watching them.

To get the greatest number of papers turned in on time, make your assignments due at the beginning of the class period. This allows students who didn't finish during the last work period to complete the project at home. It also minimizes the stress on those who have difficulty completing assignments in class.

If you have a due date at the beginning of the hour on the next day, remember to remind students about the deadline. That should be the last thing you say to them as they leave class. In addition, write it on your board in big, bold letters and have your students write it in their planners or on their arms if necessary.

Ideally when the due date arrives so does all the student work. In reality some turn the work in early, some hand it in on time, others strain to make the date, but fail, and a few make no effort at all.

Assigning Long-Range Projects

Even though we all know Rome wasn't built in a day, if the builders of that city had been middle school students, the first stones of Rome wouldn't have been laid until the day before the project was due. Students may not know how to spell *procrastination,* but they sure know how to practice it. As a result, long-range projects present quite a challenge for both students and teachers.

To make sure students complete the project on time, break the project down into smaller steps. With a writing project, the steps might be notes, outline, first draft, and final draft. Each of these steps should have its own due date, and you should remind students daily as the due dates draw near. At each step, review the students' work to make sure the objective was met. This process helps you identify those students who don't know how to do the project or who start on the wrong track.

Disciplining Students for Late or Unfinished Work

Invariably the student whose work isn't even creative enough to be considered bland will offer the most original reasons for not having his work done. After you have been teaching for a few years, you'll hear about homework papers that are chewed up by pets, disintegrated in washing machines, confiscated by bullies, thrown out bus windows, or mangled by machinery. ("I was writing it on the porch when a gust of wind blew it into the yard just as my dad came by on the riding mower.") Homework is left in cars, kitchens, jammed lockers, friends' homes, and stepparents' residences. One student even told me that his dad had shot a skunk, which expired in a furnace duct. The furnace blower spread the skunk smell to every room in the house, so the family fled the premises. The homework unfortunately was left in the student's bedroom.

Although these students get points for creativity, these excuses don't change the fact that the students need to be penalized for turning their work in late. The following sections describe increasingly harsh methods for dealing with students who don't do the work.

Dropping Grades for Late Work

The logical consequence for turning work in late is the lowering of the grade. One grade lower for each day late is a reasonable penalty for middle school or junior high students. High school teachers should consider an even steeper drop in grades.

Show the students that you're serious about wanting them to turn work in on time by developing a written assignment policy that does the following:

- Shows your grading scale
- States the penalties for late work
- Spells out how snow days or class absences affect the due date of class assignments

Share this policy with parents, review it with your classes, give your students a copy of it, and post it in the classroom. When you do this, claims of "I didn't know I would get marked down" will have no validity. Also have the late policy poster hanging in your classroom so that parents can see it when they come to visit. This takes the wind out of their sails when they are claiming that their child didn't know when the assignment was due or that there was a penalty for late work.

> **T I P** Send a copy of the policy home with students for their parents to sign. When the signed copy returns, file it. If parents question a grade at a later date, you have a signed copy of the policy to show them.

Calling Parents of Unproductive Students

Without doubt, the most effective way to get students to complete their work is to call their parents. Use the threat of a phone call as a motivator. If that doesn't work, make the call. With parents applying pressure at home while you continue to work on the student at school, academic progress may actually occur. Techniques to use when phoning parents are discussed in Chapter 17, "Working with Parents."

Raising the Specter of Saturday School

In the language arts class I taught, a book summary was due about every six weeks. Typically, only about 60 to 70 percent of the class turned in book summaries on the due date, even though papers turned in a day late dropped one grade and fell another grade if they were two days late.

To encourage more students to turn in papers on time, I announced that those who couldn't get their papers in within two days of the due date would be assigned to Saturday school. Saturday school ran from 8 to 11 on Saturday mornings at the school and was staffed by a teacher. This weekend session was designed for those who were behind in their work.

After I mentioned Saturday school, I had over 80 percent of the class hand in book summaries on time. Those who didn't found themselves back in school on the next Saturday. The thought that failing to complete an assignment might cost them part of their weekend free time proved to be a powerful incentive to make sure their work was turned in on time. One tour of duty in Saturday school usually guaranteed better scholastic performance in the weeks that followed.

Occasionally a student would refuse to attend Saturday school. In that situation, the parents and errant student had a conference with the principal. The family was told that the student would be suspended if he failed to attend Saturday school.

Sending Students to Summer School and Retaining Students

During one of my first years as a teacher I became frustrated with the number of students who failed to complete assignments. Standing in front of a class one day, I pointed out that if they didn't pass their eighth grade classes, they could end up spending a second year in eighth grade. Suddenly a hand went up, and when I called on the student, he said words to this effect:

> *"Mr. Foley, I haven't passed a class since fifth grade, and each year I get passed on to the next grade. Seriously, no one has to do this work. No matter what grades are on the report cards, they'll pass you."*

He was essentially right. I soon learned that the only students who ever repeated the grade were those whose parents requested it or those who were small for their age. I was told that retention of students doesn't work. They would only fail again if they were held back.

Studies show that this assertion is correct. Some students do passing work the second year, but most show little if any improvement.

However, the real casualties are those other students who are lazy and figure this out. Because they know they will be promoted regardless of whether they do the work, they don't apply themselves.

In my district, it seemed that each year more students were failing. The administration eventually changed its policy, adopting the idea that students who failed to pass two of their classes would be retained. The first year this policy was put into effect, the school failed 12 eighth graders. The word got around, and the next year achievement improved, and failure rates dropped. Now that there were consequences for not working, students, fearing they would have to repeat the year, began to work.

The district now informs failing students shortly after the second semester starts that if they fail two classes, they will be required to attend summer school to make up the work. If they fail summer school or do not enroll in the summer program, they repeat the grade.

Because few students are retained in the feeder middle school, when they start classes in junior high, teachers tell them right off that those who fail two or more classes must successfully complete summer school or repeat eighth grade. If they doubt the teachers, they should notice some students in their classes are in the grade for the second time. Seeing older students in their classes provides a powerful incentive to at least meet the minimum academic standard.

When I taught in that junior high school, I would mention summer school and retention periodically throughout the year. I also brought it up in phone conversations with parents of unmotivated students. A teaching colleague of mine used to remind his failing students that, *"The nice thing about this school is that every year we offer this class. If you don't pass it this year, good luck, try again next year."*

Summary

Students have to do work in order to learn. Part of a teacher's job is to encourage students do their best. The ideas presented in this chapter will help you manage your classroom so that students can be productive:

- Recognize that students work at different rates when you assign work to be finished in class. Make sure you have a plan to occupy students who finish their work early, and try to be flexible with those who need more time.

- Passing out assignment handouts and posting information in the classroom will stop some student questions about homework, but it won't eliminate all of them.

- You can stop lost homework excuses by informing students that you will mark down late work one letter grade. If that penalty doesn't motivate them to turn in their work, try a phone call to the parents, Saturday school, or even summer school or retention.

Rewarding Academic Success

Ideally students pursue education in a quest for knowledge or as a means to better understand their world. Realistically their motivations are not so lofty. An *A* on the report card, a pizza party, a chance to win some class free time, or privileges and presents from parents give them reasons to succeed with their studies. Rewards can become the flip side of discipline consequences. The loss of free time and peer pressure discussed in the first chapters of this book become sources of rewards. By understanding human nature, savvy teachers know how to get the best from their students.

Motivating the Unmotivated

Wouldn't it be wonderful if students were intrinsically motivated? If just knowing they had the opportunity to learn about the Revolutionary War, adverbs, fractions, or the composition of an atom, would be all that was needed to spur them to eagerly delve into these subjects? Research tells us what we already can figure out. Namely, students learn better when they want to learn. When students engage in an activity for its own sake, they have a higher retention of the material. Getting this to happen can be a daunting task.

Although some students pass the tests and write the papers you assign because they like school, want to get *As* and *Bs*, and are working to get into college, some aren't like that. In every class you have students who aren't motivated. They need a reason to get involved with your class.

When you try to get a student to put forth more effort with his studies, avoid mentioning reasons such as being intellectually curious, becoming an educated person, and understanding the world we live in. These reasons sound good when written into mission statements or as curriculum goals, but they are irrelevant to adolescents.

The best teachers use both intrinsic and extrinsic motivators to educate their students. Inspiring the students to learn by teaching engaging lessons or connecting with them in a personal way takes time, hard work, and creativity. Often it's easier to employ extrinsic motivators, focusing on rewards and punishments associated with learning. Finding what works is a trial-and-error process that is ongoing throughout your career in the classroom. The following sections describe some of the most effective motivators.

Likeable Teachers

A good place to start is with you, the teacher. Although it is well known that elementary age children are dedicated teacher pleasers, this phenomenon continues to some extent on into junior and senior high years. If students perceive you as a good person, they might do their best work for no other reason than to please you. Chapter 9, "Connecting with Your Students" explains what you can do to become a teacher that students want to please.

Interesting Class Activities

To succeed in getting genuine enthusiasm for learning, establish a pleasant learning environment by trying to make class enjoyable by incorporating fun projects and activities into your lesson plans. Here are some ideas:

- **Play a game.** Adolescents love to compete. In the process of trying to help their team to win, actual learning may happen. This idea is described in more detail later in the chapter.

> **T I P** Remember what you want students to learn and then make sure that the game helps you to achieve that goal. Sometimes there is so much emphasis on the playing of the game that the academic objective is lost.

- **Put students in charge.** Perhaps the best way to get students interested in the lesson is to put them in charge of creating it. You can even get good results by letting your class write its own test.

- **Chant key concepts.** To encourage class participation, have the class repeat an important fact after you. For example, many of my students would mistakenly identify the word *not* as a verb, so I had them repeat the sentence, "Not is never a verb." Students love to mimic teachers, so have the class say the fact fast, slow, in a high voice, in a low voice, and in any voice you can think of. You can even have them sing the fact. After repeating the fact 10 or 15 times in a variety of voice inflections, your students will be unlikely to forget the fact you're trying to teach.

- **Make students idea messengers.** Instruct students to say a fact you want them to remember to five people during the next 24 hours. For example, because I was frustrated that so many of my students kept listing adverbs as verbs, I had them say, "*L Y* words are never verbs." The people can be family members, friends, people who work at the school, or even strangers. The next day, have students share stories of how these people reacted when the students said the seemingly nonsensical phrase.

All it takes to create an engaging lesson plan or exercise is a motivated teacher. If you're not the creative type, there are Internet lessons, textbooks, and magazine articles available that are full of ideas.

Entertainment

Comatose classes don't learn. Humor works. Injecting a joke or adding a quirky observation into a presentation keeps students alert, raising the possibility that some education will occur.

I found it easy to inject humor into most activities. For example, to make grammar more palatable, I would often substitute my own sample sentences for the ones listed in the textbook. Mine were nonsensical and aimed at the type of humor appreciated by adolescents. These sentences elicited chuckles and smiles as the students identified the parts of speech. Whenever I gave a multiple-choice test, option D was always totally absurd. The tests may have been challenging, but no one ever found them boring.

Although I would do my best to build interest in required material whenever I could, sometimes I would break away briefly from lecturing to do something to entertain the class. Telling a joke, making a wry observation, or serving up a one-liner usually recaptured the students' attention. If the joke related to the lesson that was excellent, but even if it didn't, when students laughed or looked startled I knew they were listening. If the joke was memorable, they would alert their friends outside the class to what I had done, and the classes later in the day would be more likely to play close attention because they heard something funny was going to happen.

If I saw that students were interested or amused by something I did, I did it every hour that day. If a lesson went well, then I stayed with that presentation all day. If I was losing them or seeing signs of boredom, I tried to tweak the plan for subsequent classes, hoping to better catch their attention.

Most of the funny things that I said or did in class were unscripted and spontaneous. Rarely did I know what I was going to do. Yet suddenly as I was teaching, something weird or funny would occur to me and I would have to share it with the class. Usually by the time I got home at night I had forgotten the laugh-getter. Apparently my students hadn't, because years later when I would see these kids as adults, they would tell me about something I did or said when they were in my class. I usually had no memory of it at all. As children of my first students were assigned to my class, I would be asked to repeat a joke I had done some 20 years earlier.

The Surefire Cure for Academic Apathy

To an adolescent, the future is this afternoon, tomorrow, or maybe next weekend. A college education? A rewarding career? These events will occur so far in the future that junior high students can't even conceive of when they will happen. They will give lip service to these ideas, but these goals are not priorities. Hanging out with their friends after school, buying the latest video game, and making the eighth grade basketball team are what's important to them. The school is a mandatory collection point, allowing adolescents a legitimate way to escape their homes and be with their friends. They tolerate classes as necessary blocks of time between social time in the halls and lunchroom. They don't dislike the academics of school and readily give testimony to the importance of getting an education, but it's just hard to focus on that when there is so much social stimulation and adolescent anxiety to deal with. Math, science, language arts, and social studies can't compete with those other attractions. Underachieving is the norm.

However, I have found a surefire cure for academic apathy. To prove my point, I used to present the following scenario to the class: "Suppose I said to you that Michigan State University was funding an experiment dealing with student motivation and had contacted me. The people doing the experiment will pay 10 dollars to every student who can get a B or better on next week's grammar test. Those students who got a B or B+ on the last test must raise their grade to an A to get the money. They've asked me to determine how much money they should set aside for the payout. I want you to be totally honest with me. Don't raise your hand unless you are sure you can qualify for the money. Okay, how many of you can get a B or raise your last B to an A this time? Raise your hand." Nearly all the hands would go up. I got the same response every time I presented this scenario.

Nothing would get students' interest better than a chance to earn some cash. People in one to one conversations with students have found that students will try harder when money is offered. That tells me that students will do better if the right motivation is offered. Experts complain about low test scores, failing schools, the lack of learning, and the schools' inability to solve those problems. I think the solution is simple: Pay the kids.

Preparation for High School

One thing I used to hear occasionally from my students was that grades in junior high don't count, so they didn't plan to start working until they were freshmen in high school. When students made these statements, I talked to them using as an example an interest of theirs, such as band or a specific sport, in a conversation similar to the following:

> Teacher: *"Jim, you like basketball, don't you? Do you want to play on the varsity squad in your junior year? Are you playing basketball now?"*
>
> Jim: "Yes."
>
> Teacher: *"But it doesn't count now. Your varsity tryout isn't for three years. Why are you playing now?"*
>
> Jim: "I have to practice now, so I'll be good enough to make the team when the tryouts come."
>
> Teacher: *"Could the same thing be true with going to college? If you don't learn your grammar and develop your writing skills now, you won't be able to do well next year when the grades are going to count."*

They understood the sports analogy because it was real to them. Students knew that those who worked hard at sports made the team, so it made sense to work at English in middle school "when the grades didn't count" in order to do better in future years when grades mattered.

Rewards and Punishments from Parents and Teachers

On the home front, parents may get their offspring to perform by creating monetary incentives or offering privileges for getting good grades. Negative reinforcements also are effective. Students will keep an eye on their grades to avoid being grounded or losing use of the Internet, television, or telephone.

When students are not motivated, the parents' role can be crucial. If parents are effectively monitoring their child's work, as well as offering rewards or penalties based on productivity, the teacher's job can become easier. And although parents may talk to their child about getting into college, landing a good job, and making enough money to live comfortably, they realize these bits of wisdom aren't the motivating factors. Whether the work gets done well and turned in on time depends on what incentives and penalties the parents have set up. (This topic is discussed in greater detail in Chapter 17, "Working with Parents.")

The same system works well in the classroom as opportunities are created to exchange favors for improved student academic performance or penalties are levied for low productivity. When offered incentives, individuals and whole classes will work harder.

Accelerating Learning to Earn Free Time

Essentially you teach a concept until your students master it. To achieve mastery often requires doing repetitive exercises, drills, and question-and-answer sessions until the students know the concepts. Too often the material doesn't seem relevant. Consequently there is a noticeable lack of zeal in response to your efforts. It approximates the maxim, "You can lead a horse to water, but you can't make it drink."

To get students interested, make it worth their while. Because you are operating in a school setting, your options are limited. However, one reward is a sure thing, and that is an offer to end the lesson. This reward works well when you are doing work orally. Alternatively, you can reward students by switching to a class activity they enjoy more.

The first step is to give the class a goal. For example, you might say, *"Let's do these 20 problems. Or better yet, we'll quit the exercise as soon as you can get 15 correct."* Now everybody is working hard to get 15 problems correct so the class can quit doing problems. With this kind of enthusiasm and focus, the students will learn more by doing 15 problems instead of all 20. You can adapt this tactic to almost any curriculum, and you can do it in a variety of ways.

> **TIP** Don't make the goal too easy or too hard. If it's attainable, your students will go for it.

Competing for Academic Excellence

Adolescents love to compete, but physical education class doesn't need to be the only situation where they have spirited contests. Classroom competitions, wherein students work frantically to recall details of an assignment or have to demonstrate mastery of the lesson to earn points, channel natural adolescent energy in a positive way. Although the lesson itself may not excite your students, they will be more interested in learning the material if knowing the material will help them win a battle of the sexes or another competition. Winning can be its own reward, or you can award free time as a prize.

> **TIP** If you have an unequal number of girls and boys, then have each row of desks be a team or one side of the room compete against the other.

To make sure that some students won't sit out and let the brainy kids answer all the questions, figure out a system that will randomize your selections so that every student will need to be prepared to answer a question. Without making it obvious to your class, try to pitch easier questions to those who are less capable so they will feel like they can succeed.

By examining lesson plans, you usually can figure a way to turn part of it into a game. For example, when I taught social studies, identifying geographic features on a map was a key curriculum objective. At the end of the week, the class played Speed Geography. Two students stood about 10 feet out from a pull-down map of the world. When I named a place, they would race to be the first to touch that spot on the map. Their classmates could offer information. At times the game was chaotic, as players made desperate leaps to get their hand on the place first while classmates shouted out help. By frequently changing players who stood before the map and encouraging those at their seats to participate, I was able to involve almost everyone in this lesson.

> T I P Adolescents are energetic beings, ready to respond to any stimuli. Class activities that give adolescents the chance to move about or raise their voices enable them to release their pent-up energy in a productive way.

For the study of state geography, I gave everyone a road map. This time when I asked about the location of a place, everyone looked on their road map, raising their hands when they found the answer. Although the students eventually became proficient at identifying the cities and rivers on the map, they were horribly inept at folding the map. To add a little spice to the lesson at the end of the hour, the class had a map folding competition to see who could get the map folded correctly first. Looking at my watch, I gave the command "Go," and they began to fold. The air filled with the sound of crinkling paper. As the students folded their maps correctly, they held them up, and I read off the time. It was a win-win situation. My maps were folded correctly, and my students had fun.

Using Peer Pressure for Class Success

Lacking the cash to provide the one surefire cure for underachieving, I tried a different approach. Maybe peer pressure would be my ally. If I offered a class a reward, perhaps the students would work harder so they wouldn't let their classmates down. Likewise, threatening a class with a penalty might encourage some underachievers to work a little harder so that the class can avoid the penalty. Knowing that junior high students would do almost anything to get out of work, I also found that students could sometimes learn more by doing less.

Rewarding a Higher Class Grade Average

I decided to test my class reward theory with an essay-writing project. I always do this assignment right after Christmas break when theoretically students' minds are fresh after two weeks of intellectual inactivity. By looking over grade books from other years, I did some calculations and discovered that class averages for this project on a four-point scale typically were about 2.5. Going to a 2.75 average didn't seem too hard, and it would represent significant improvement.

The first day back after break, I offered these rewards for getting a class average of 2.75 on the essay project:

1. The students would not have to do the next assigned book report.

2. Because the students were all going to be trying harder, this essay would count twice as much as a typical writing assignment.

3. The students would get a free class hour where they could watch television or play games. (The free hour was amazing to them because I never had free days. I was never one for showing movies, offering snacks, or just blowing a class hour. Even on the last day before a holiday break, the best I would offer was a reading day.)

For two weeks the class prepared the essay; they wrote, corrected, and made final copies. The students worked more intently than they usually did. Sometimes they seemed almost enthusiastic. Even the most apathetic students picked up their pencils and started scribbling. No one wanted to incur the disapproval of his or her classmates by being seen as a slacker. Meanwhile I kept reminding the students of the incentives and wrote them on one corner of the board.

On the due date, only 4 papers were missing out of 138. As I graded the essays, I noticed that many students had produced their best work of the year. In particular, my least talented writers showed notable improvement. Students who never seemed to have much to contribute came through with thoughts that were excellent. When I tallied the scores, four of my five classes achieved the 2.75 standard, and one edged above 2.8. The next day my classes watched movies and the television show *Crocodile Hunter*. One class played Twister.

Penalizing the Class for Late Work

Because all my students watched the clock, I would sometimes use covering the clock face as a means of getting more student work completed. One day, for example, I posted a notice beside the clock that read, "Eighty percent or the clock gets covered." The response was immediate and frantic. You would think I said all the computers and televisions in the world were about to be destroyed.

I told them that all I was asking of them was to hand their next book summaries in on time. Usually I received 60 to 70 percent on the due date. However, only 55 percent had arrived on the last due date. The students had six weeks to read a book and summarize it in 150 words, so I figured it wasn't unreasonable to ask for 80 percent of the students to turn in their work on time. Until a class had turned in 80 percent of the book summaries, a sheet of cardboard would cover the clock face. Students who wore watches, which few students did, were allowed to check the time, but telling the time to any other class members was forbidden.

When the due date arrived, two classes made the 80 percent; three didn't. An appointed Officer of the Clock taped the cardboard over the clock face at the start of the hour, and the delinquent classes labored in a timeless world. "How many more reports need to come in to get us to 80 percent?" they would ask. And I would tell them. Peer pressure did the rest. By the end of a week, enough delinquent book summaries came in to help the other three classes reach 80 percent, and we all were clock-watchers again.

Rewarding Work with Less Work

Every day in my language arts class the first thing the class did was a warm-up exercise. On the board I wrote two sentences containing grammatical errors. The students copied these sentences and made corrections. (The exercise is called the Daily Oral Language or DOL and is an exercise book used in many school districts.) While they were doing this, I could take attendance without interruption. After about five minutes, we corrected the exercise. It was a routine. As soon as they walked into the classroom, they started copying the sentences. Although we did the DOL about 95 percent of the time, the chance to avoid doing it was a powerful incentive to get the students to work.

For example, the class had been working on career research all week. Although a few students were done, many hadn't finished, so the class needed some time to complete their work. I was concerned that the students who had already finished or who finished before the end of the class would become restless and distract the ones who were still working. I had reminded students to bring their books to read for their book summaries, but I felt they might need an extra incentive to stay quiet. On the board I wrote, *"Don't do the DOL today. The third time I ask the class to be quiet, we'll do the DOL."* By offering a chance to avoid the DOL as a reward, I got their cooperation. The students wanted the classroom to be quiet so they could get out of doing the DOL. Typically at least one class would get the third warning, and those students, of course, had to do the DOL. When I gave the third warning, I also named the offender. This student got dirty looks and sometimes a rebuke from his classmates. This type of negative peer response often helped such students to improve their behavior.

Sometimes I had a lesson planned that would take the full class period, and I didn't want to give up the five minutes needed to do the DOL. Such lessons were a great opportunity to offer to give up DOL as a reward. On those days, I announced that if the students would give me their full attention and work well during the full class period, they wouldn't have to do the DOL. I cautioned that if they became restless, the deal was off. Usually this strategy worked. I may have had to point to the DOL sentences once or twice and say, *"Are we going to have to do the DOL?"* as a reminder, but generally the class was cooperative.

I noticed that junior high students would also behave to get an extension of a deadline. If a composition or project was due on a Tuesday, I might offer to move the deadline back a day if they worked efficiently without causing disruption on Monday. When I did these kinds of deals, I had peer pressure working in my favor. The students wanted the extra time, and they were quick to get on any kid whose behavior would jeopardize their chance for a deadline extension. Obviously if the students didn't behave, they had to complete the assignment for the original due date; otherwise, my credibility would have been shot.

> T I P Don't offer deadline extensions on a regular basis, or students will expect them. Keep most of your original deadlines, and surprise your students with opportunities to get additional time to work.

Once students realize you might cancel exercises or extend deadlines, they will ask you every day, "Can we skip the assignment today?" or "Can we have another day on our projects?" To avoid these daily pleadings, the first time you change a deadline or cancel an assignment, make this statement:

"If you ask if the class can skip the assignment or have a deadline extended, I won't do it. And if I was thinking of it and you ask, I won't do it. I want it to be a surprise."

I know that sounds dumb, but if you don't say something like that, I guarantee that the first thing you'll hear every class period of every day is "Can we skip the assignment today?"

Summary

Although classroom management strategies are usually applied to change student behavior, the same techniques can be used to help students become better learners. Remember these key points as you try to motivate your students to learn:

- Try to make your class enjoyable as well as educational.

- Any time you can make a game or competition out of learning, students will usually work hard to master the lesson so that their team will win.

- To encourage your students to work hard, set goals for them and offer rewards such as free time if they meet those goals.

- If you occasionally extend a deadline or cancel an assignment, you'll be amazed how hard junior high students will work to avoid work.

CHAPTER 14

Managing Your Classroom

When one thinks about classroom management, the first thing that comes to mind is a need for developing a system for managing the behavior of students. So teachers focus on being ready to handle all kinds of student misbehaviors. However, if you think of classroom management as actually managing the classroom setting, you can create an environment where misbehavior is less likely to happen. This chapter presents techniques for making your classroom operate more efficiently.

Planning Your Lessons

When you are teaching, students tend to behave well. Likewise, if you assign them a task and are monitoring them, they cooperate. It is the downtime that students can't handle. During those unstructured moments that occur while you take attendance, talk to a student, look for your notes, retrieve something from a file cabinet, or write notes on the board, the talking and fooling around starts.

As mentioned in Chapter 5, sometimes it doesn't hurt to let students talk. However, when you present the lesson, you want them to behave. If you stop to hunt around for a book or to write a paragraph on the board, they will become restless. By the time you settle them down again, they will lose the thread of what you were teaching, and you may not remember exactly what point you were making when you suddenly had to switch roles from an educator to a class manager.

> **TIP** Have the materials you will need for your lesson on hand at the start of class. All manner of chaos may erupt while you have your head buried in a file cabinet looking for a handout.

Think ahead about what materials you need for class and what activities you will be doing so you can prepare before your students arrive in the classroom. Have all handouts and book references marked ahead of time, as well as all materials written on the board. This preparation helps lessons to go smoothly so that all you have to be concerned about is teaching the lesson and keeping your students on task. The following sections describe different ways you can prepare yourself and your class so that you can be an effective teacher.

Knowing the Lesson

To keep a class under control, you have to have lesson plans that engage students. You can do very little to control a class when your instruction is ineffective. When you thoroughly know your material and exactly how you are going to teach a lesson, you are able to effectively monitor your students' behavior.

Soon after I became a teacher, I discovered that the days I had the most trouble controlling my students were the days that my lesson plans were shaky. If I was hesitant in my delivery because I wasn't sure what I was doing, then it became doubly hard to keep my students in line as I struggled not only with their behavior, but also with trying to figure out how to teach the lesson.

Avoiding Technological Difficulties

If you have a lesson that relies on technology, make sure that the equipment needed, be it CD player, DVD player, or television, is operable. In addition, if you are relying on computers, check that they are working and that the Internet connection and Web sites you need are working. Have a backup lesson plan in place as well, in case the electronic wizardry goes on the fritz.

When teachers use technology, Murphy's Law is in full operation: "Anything that can go wrong will go wrong." For example, every teacher has a horror story about the school's copy machine. Only a fool or a gambler waits until the last minute to run off copies needed for the day's lesson. The joke in the teacher's lounge is that all you need to do to shut down a school district is to disable all the copy machines.

Preventing Burnout

School years are 9 to 10 months long. Few teachers can go full blast through the entire year. By alternating between challenging or stressful teaching units and less strenuous ones, you will not be totally spent by the time the spring months come.

As a language arts teacher, when I did my two-week essay writing unit, it demanded my full attention and culminated with five classes of papers to correct. By the end of the unit, I was worn out. The next week, rather than jumping into another major project, I would ease back and switch over to something easier, such as reading and discussing a short story, which would allow me to recover before embarking on the next writing project.

Preparing for Special Events

Veteran teachers learn to anticipate the ramifications of every new situation. This way of thinking may seem obvious when the class leaves the classroom for a field trip or to attend an assembly. For these events, teachers always have a plan. For example, every teacher always recites the assembly rules before the students leave the classroom:

> *"Remember class, we don't boo, whistle, kick the seat in front of us, put paper in people's hair, or clap continuously at the end so you won't have to go to your next class."*

With middle school or junior high students, you don't have to leave the classroom to get surprises. Anything out of the ordinary will get them going. So if you're planning a lab class, a guest speaker, a cooperative learning exercise, or oral presentations, try to imagine what effect that activity will have on your students and prepare them for it.

Starting Class

The first minutes of your class aren't for teaching anymore. They are for taking attendance, signing passes, answering urgent student requests, or doing any number of odd tasks. To keep students busy during this time, try a warm-up exercise that doesn't require you to stand in front of the class. Depending on what you teach, you might have a math problem, grammar exercise, question of the day, a quiz, or a read-and-respond activity. As long as the class can do it without instruction, explanation, or assistance, you will get your five minutes to handle the start-up stuff, and the students will have something to focus their attention on.

Providing Instructions

It's inevitable that as soon as you make a statement such as, "You're going to write an essay," several hands will go up, and someone will immediately say, "When is it due?" while someone else interrupts to ask, "How long does it have to be?" followed by a, "Can we pick our own topic?" and then a, "Does it have to be typed?" If you start answering these questions, more will come, and those asking questions won't be listening to your answers, so they'll ask the same question that you just answered.

However, there's a simple solution to avoiding this game of many questions. Before you introduce the topic or assignment, say, *"There will be no questions until after I'm done with my instructions. Then I will answer any questions you have."* This statement eliminates lots of interruptions and still gives the students a chance to ask questions. The following sections explain other strategies you can use to avoid answering the same questions class after class.

> TIP If students will be working in groups that they select, don't divulge this information until you have given all other instructions. Otherwise, they'll be so intently looking around and signaling who they want to work with that they will totally tune you out.

Writing Instructions

Yes, finding ways to engage your students in conversations does help build rapport with them; however, answering the question "What are we doing today?" a half-dozen times at the beginning of each class period seems to erode some of the joy of student-staff interaction. Day in and day out, year in and year out, the same questions come at you ad nauseum:

"When is the book report due?"

"Do we have to skip lines?"

"What happens if I turn my report in late?"

"What time does this class get out?"

"Can I write it in pencil?"

The solution to this problem is to write out the answers to the most commonly asked questions and post them in the room where everyone can see them. Post information that is useful all year, such as the proper heading for a paper or your policy on late work.

Writing the simplest instructions for the daily lesson on the board can save you from having to say the same thing over and over. As you start a lesson, first wait until everyone sees you and is quiet. Then say the instructions as you write the key information on the board. Now those who weren't listening won't have to ask you to repeat the assignment.

Finally, it's a good idea to develop handouts for information that students will need to refer to all year and for specific assignments. Such handouts can summarize a lesson that might not be found in the textbook or among student resources or can serve as quick review sheets. You can give them to students who missed the lecture or were absent from school when the lesson was presented. For example, I created an information sheet about essay writing called "The Well-Written Essay," included in this chapter. Shorter instruction sheets for specific assignments are also useful. You can give these sheets to students who were absent when the assignment was given and parents who want to help their children with assignments. (I have included an example of this type of handout, titled "Writing a Good Essay," in this chapter for your reference.)

Posting Lesson Plans

Writing a daily schedule of what you will be doing in class on the board will head off a lot of those "What are we doing today?" questions. Some teachers even post a week-in-brief listing of what will be accomplished each day. These listings are effective if you stick to the agenda; however, students rarely learn at exactly the rate specified in the lesson plans. Typically when Friday arrived, my students were still trying to master the lesson I planned to finish on Wednesday. On rare occasions, they gobbled up the material so fast that they completed Friday's lesson on Thursday. In any event, the five-day plan the students first saw on the board Monday quickly became obsolete.

Unless you are erasing and rewriting every day, your students may try to use what you had written initially as an excuse for doing the wrong assignment on the wrong day or missing a deadline. It might be better to just stick with a daily written notice of what the class will be doing and verbally tell the class what you hope will be accomplished during the week rather than putting up a five-day plan.

The Well-Written Essay

Essays explore (analyze), explain, or argue.

Prewriting

Begin by brainstorming and writing down possible topics that come to your mind. Focus in on one or two topics that seem interesting to you and that you know something about.

At this point, select a topic and start forming questions that you might want to answer, using the words *what, where, why, when,* and *how.* This process helps you discover areas that you might want to explore in your essay. Write down examples you could use to illustrate the points you want to make.

At regular intervals ask, "What am I trying to say?" and then answer the question in your mind or on the paper. Look at your subject from different angles. When you feel that you have enough information to write the essay, you are ready to write an introduction.

The Introduction

An essay begins with an opening statement that captures the reader's attention. Avoid bland beginnings, such as "I am going to write about what it means to take things for granted." Instead, try something like this:

"Shivering in the drizzling rain, my numb fingers awkwardly fumbled with the match in a futile attempt to light the pile of damp wood. Without a cooking fire, dinner would be just a handful of M&Ms. I realized then how much I take for granted. I think simple things like dry clothes, a place to get out of the rain, and hot food will always be available. On my summer wilderness canoeing trips, I learned to go without many things that most people take for granted."

Note that in the fourth sentence I gave a definition ("I think simple things...will always be available.") in case people didn't know what it means to take things for granted. Whereas the preceding paragraph attempts to capture the readers' interest by citing a part of a narrative, there are other ways to capture a reader's interest, such as this example of an introductory paragraph:

continued

continued

"In the twenty-first century, we take many things for granted that our parents and grandparents didn't have. Modern conveniences such as microwaves, DVD players, cell phones, iPods, and leaf blowers weren't available a quarter century ago. A wilderness canoe trip takes you even farther back into time, as you must often do without conveniences that have been with us for a hundred years. Last summer on a trip into Canada's backcountry, I became acutely aware of just how much I take for granted."

The Body of the Essay

Working from your prewriting notes, select a point that helps explain your topic and write a paragraph wherein you'll explain this point and give an example to clarify it. Typically you'll have at least three points to make and thus three paragraphs to create. The main idea in each paragraph must relate directly to the topic and give information to better explain your thesis. (Remember that a *thesis* tells the purpose of your paper.)

In the case of the topic of taking things for granted, the idea of the conveniences absent from a wilderness trip would be developed. Perhaps you might start with a paragraph explaining how the wilderness food and cooking methods differ from cooking at home. Another section might talk about having to cope with weather in the wilderness. And the third might talk about how campers become chief mechanics and doctors because there is no one to call for help if a problem occurs.

As you are writing the body of the essay, include transitions so the sentences flow from one idea to another and make the transitions from paragraph to paragraph smooth. Here is where glue words are helpful. [Our grammar text referred to coordinating, correlative, and subordinating conjunctions as *glue words*.]

Conclusion

Finish with a summarizing statement wherein you tie key points together or emphasize an especially important idea.

Revising

While proofreading, in addition to correcting mechanical and grammatical errors, add descriptive words and rewrite awkward or weak sentences.

Writing a Good Essay

An essay is a paper in which you discuss a topic so others can learn what you think about this topic.

Here are the steps to follow:

1. Select a topic that interests you. Here are some topic ideas: facing a challenge, dealing with pressure, being a team player, patriotism, loyalty, honesty, doing the right thing, being responsible, peer pressure, friendship, being a role model, conformity, setting goals, being mature, and leadership.

2. Write out several questions about the topic. Here I have used sportsmanship as a sample topic:

   What does it mean to practice good sportsmanship?

   How can people demonstrate good sportsmanship?

   Why is important to show good sportsmanship?

   What are some examples of good sportsmanship?

   When have I seen good sportsmanship?

3. Write about experiences that are examples of your topic. These experiences are often things that you witnessed or that happened to you. Your answers to the topic questions as well as the examples you use to explain your points will provide the information you will use in your rough draft.

4. Begin writing your rough draft. Start with an **introduction** paragraph that tells what you are going to write about and catches the reader's interest. Next is the **body** of your essay, which should be at least three paragraphs. Each paragraph describes a different point you are making about your topic and gives an example to illustrate that point. The **conclusion** paragraph wraps up loose ends of your essay and summarizes (or makes a concluding statement) about your topic.

5. After you have read your rough draft out loud and corrected grammar and spelling errors, begin writing your final draft.

Avoiding Problems in Lab Classes

Artists mold clay; adolescents want to throw it. Scientists examine worms; middle school boys want to scare girls with them. Artists enjoy painting on canvas whereas junior high students enjoy painting each other. Art and science teachers must channel this student energy toward producing artwork and science experiments while at the same time thwarting adolescents' mischievous tendencies. This is not an easy task.

Most of the mischief that goes on in lab classes occurs when students

- Don't know what they are supposed to do
- Fear their results won't be impressive
- Act out to get attention

Success in lab classes starts with meticulous planning. You must thoroughly know how to teach the lesson, what materials will be needed, and how long the lesson will take. The time needed for cleanup must also be factored in.

The lesson starts with you explaining and perhaps demonstrating how the science experiment or art project is done. The students should be sitting facing you with nothing but a blank work surface in front of them, unless they are taking notes. To put art supplies or lab equipment at hand would be too distracting for some in your audience. Spell out the project in a step-by-step manner. In addition, give the students a handout or write directions on the board to save yourself from having to repeat the instructions countless times.

Just before passing out the items to be used in the project, talk about safety concerns and remind students what behavior is inappropriate. Warn them of the disciplinary action that will befall all who dare ignore any safety concerns or use materials and equipment in any manner other than that for which they were intended. A lab teacher's tolerance for misbehavior must be low. Once you've issued all the necessary stuff, you must never leave the room or turn your back on the class for more than a millisecond. That's why it is vital that you plan ahead and have everything you need ready before the experiment or art project starts.

Cleanup is a group project. Encourage cooperation by issuing this edict, *"No one will leave until the room is clean."* If groups are in their own workstations, seated around a table, for instance, then they may be held responsible for just their area. Before a class or group is dismissed, the students should sit in their seats while you inspect the area.

Because items like utility knives, markers, scissors, glue sticks, and scalpels are attractive to students, theft can be a problem. Therefore, you need to know exactly how many and what kind of objects are issued to each work group. Putting each group's supplies into a colored box with a list of contents taped to the outside makes it easier to ensure all items are returned at the end of class. Make sure you account for all items before you dismiss the students.

Keeping Students Focused

Meeting curriculum objectives and achieving student mastery of basic skills involves drills and repetitive activities that can be tedious. Teachers can improve the lessons with innovations and with creative presentations, but it's hard to get away from sessions where the teacher is up front and the students are responding. Typically the exercise might be doing a series of math problems, identifying words in a grammar exercise, or answering content questions. The teacher might be calling on student volunteers, picking respondents randomly, or correcting homework orally. In any event, sometimes it becomes apparent that although physically 30 bodies are in the class, some students have mentally checked out.

> TIP When you're teaching, stand in front of the class and make eye contact with your class. Students never seem to be able to hear you unless they can see you. Standing in close proximity to troublemakers also helps hold their attention.

To get everyone back on task, you can utilize several strategies:

- Offer students an incentive that will reward the class for staying on task. For example, if the exercise involves 15 questions, offer them the option of doing only 10 if every time you call on someone that person knows exactly what problem is being done.

- Students invariably would rather do a lesson orally than have to write it out. With this in mind, offer them the opportunity to do the work orally as long as everyone is on task.

- Tell the class that as soon as they get a certain percentage right or provide several consecutive correct answers the lesson will end.

Although there will always be students with their hands raised ready to answer questions, don't rely strictly on them. Otherwise, the rest of the class has no incentive to pay attention. Make sure a certain number of respondents are randomly selected. While leading the discussion or doing the lesson, calling on those who seem distracted or daydreaming will quickly get them focused on what the class is doing. Telling the class as the exercise starts that students who get called on but don't know which question is being answered will be disciplined also helps keep everyone on task.

Making Sure Students Understand the Lesson

Teaching is easy. Ensuring that students are learning is the hard part. What generally results is partial learning, meaning that some of what is taught is learned while other material needs to be retaught. To sort this out, teachers give practice exercises or quizzes. However, determining exactly what parts need to be retaught is difficult. Nevertheless, there is a way to quickly discover just what material the class hasn't mastered. It's called the beep system.

Start by giving the class a quiz, review exercise, or homework, making sure that the individual questions cover the concepts the students need to know. Then have the students exchange their finished papers.

A Teacher's Attention-Getting Behavior

Being the track coach meant that in the spring students came to my room to pick up a physical exam card and a urine specimen cup, which they were to fill and carry, along with the card, to their physical exam. Beside my desk, therefore, were a stack of physical cards and a box of plastic cups. During one lunch hour, I partially filled one specimen cup with Mountain Dew, carried it back to my room, and set it on my desk.

As soon as the students in my next class saw that specimen cup with the yellow liquid in it, they asked the obvious question, "Where did that come from?" I told them someone must have mistakenly turned the sample in to me instead of his doctor, at which point I began the day's lesson. For the next 50 minutes, I led a spirited discussion on some facet of English. As I finished, I took the cap off the cup and downed the liquid. Eyes widened, and jaws dropped. Several students stammered, "Mr. Foley!" and "What did you do?"

To which I replied, "After all that talking my mouth got kind of dry." Moments later the bell rang, and I waved them off to their next class.

A stunt like this definitely will give you a reputation for being a little off-the-wall, but it also keeps your students interested. They are always wondering what you will do next. When you have their attention, your job as teacher becomes a little easier.

Begin reading off the answers, but stop after each answer. After giving an answer, ask all the students who are correcting a paper that has that item wrong to say, "Beep." If you have a chorus of beeps, obviously your students need help with that concept. You can then take a minute to explain how to arrive at the right answer. It helps if each student can look at the test question as well as the answer. In this way students can see how to answer the question correctly. When you give an answer and don't hear any beeps, assume that the students don't need reteaching of that item.

The beep system enables you to be more effective, because you won't need to spend time on concepts that the students have mastered. In addition, the beep system (although chirps or other sound effects can substituted for beeps) is popular with middle school and junior high students.

Improving Performance on Standardized Tests

Standardized tests can appear to be a no-win situation. Low-performing students may find many items that are impossible for them to do. Top students, used to being able to completely master material, may be frustrated that they can't achieve perfection. However, it is important that all students do their best.

To help students improve their performance, teachers should start preparations for the test several weeks before the test is administered. Having classes do practice exercises involving similar formats to the test will help them get comfortable with test procedures and exam question styles. Tell the students that they should try to answer all questions and that the exercises are timed. Emphasize that they should answer the questions that they know first, and then they should go back and work on other questions. If they have time left over, encourage them to check their work, especially difficult questions.

Never use questions from the test, nor should you teach specific information that will be included on the test. Although lessons may encompass general concepts that are important to know and will be utilized in the test, you should never "teach to the test."

Using Hall Passes

Figuring out a system for dealing with hall passes is something that faces every teacher. Although one might be tempted to just deny all requests for passes, this approach is unpractical. Bathroom emergencies do occur, and those students need to leave the classroom. On the other hand, if you grant all requests, you will have a constant stream of students coming and going. If you decide that only one student can be out of the room at a time, it's guaranteed that most of the time someone will be gone.

Instead, address the issue in one of your first class sessions. Explain that leaving the classroom is a privilege and not a right. The teacher has the right to deny any requests. Go on to explain that there are situations when a student needs to leave and those requests will be honored. However, students who attempt to get a pass almost every day should be careful because they are most likely to be denied a pass. (School-issued planners usually have a hall pass check sheet which will give you some idea of how frequently students are leaving class.) Also, make it a policy that when you are lecturing or working directly with students that hall pass requests will be granted only if the situation is dire.

The teacher in the classroom next to mine had another way of dealing with this issue. He limited his students to three passes in a semester. Even though his classes complained about his edict, there was never any evidence of students having "accidents" in his classroom.

Sometimes you'll doubt that a student really needs to go to the bathroom, but you certainly do not want to deny a student who truly is in an emergency situation. In this case, grant permission, but ask the student to sign her name on the board on the way out to signify that she will stay a minute after class. Miraculously most problems evaporate at that point, and the student will decide that she didn't have to go that badly.

> T I P Use bathroom passes as a bartering chip for good behavior or improved academic performance. Communicate to classes that those who disrupt class or fail to demonstrate good study habits won't get passes.

Tracking Student Work

On the first day of school, I would look at the expanse of brown laminated plastic that was my desktop. Without some concerted effort on my part, that clear, flat surface would soon disappear under a flood of student papers, administrative memos, staff bulletins, and junk mail. During my first years of teaching, I struggled to stay ahead of the paper chase by piling, filing, and pitching paper in a futile attempt to develop a coherent system of organization.

Inevitably, some student papers were lost. Well, they were not really lost; *misplaced* would be a better word. The problem was that when I needed to have them, they weren't there. Only rarely did they actually disappear. Instead, they would migrate in with the papers from another class, slip under my planbook, or find their way into a stack of daily bulletins. Things improved immensely when I set a green plastic box on my desk and required student portfolios.

The In Box

On one corner of my desk sat a green plastic box. Every student assignment that came in went into that box. No exceptions. Each piece of work had the student's name on it, the hour he was in class, the date, and the name of the assignment. I made it clear to the students that all papers must go into the green box and nowhere else. (Even though my organization was better, my desktop was sometimes still mounded with papers, but at least student work was not mixed in with the clutter.)

I emptied the box daily, usually each hour, but definitely before I left class at the end of the day. Emptying the box often was important because late work received a lower grade so I needed to know on what day the work was turned in. When I removed papers from the box, I then clipped them together and put them on a shelf behind my desk. I almost always corrected these papers on the day they were turned in.

After I corrected the papers, I recorded the grades and sorted the papers by class hour. Then I put them into file folders. I had one folder prepared for each hour. When I handed the students' work back to them after we had gone over the work, I passed out student portfolios, and the students filed their work in their individual portfolios.

The Value of Portfolios

In my school district, staff members are required to make sure students maintain portfolios, which are passed along with the students as they advance through their high school years. Having student work in portfolios helps staff make assessments regarding student placement and enables teachers of incoming students to get a better understanding of those students' strengths and weaknesses in class work.

Portfolios also provide a backup in the event that grades are contested or the computer grade book crashes and disappears into cyberspace. In addition, during parent conferences, teachers can produce the actual papers to verify grades and show the parent how a particular grade was determined. When I taught, each class had a box containing the portfolios for that group, so if a question about student work came up, I could find the portfolio almost immediately.

Remembering What You Usually Forget

You write the major stuff, such as departmental meetings and parent conferences, in your planner; it's the little stuff that you can forget to do. You get a message to call a parent during your conference hour. Ron, who's supposed to stay after class, sneaks out. You give Jennie a one-day extension on an assignment. How are you going to remember to call that parent on your conference hour, make sure Ron is disciplined for skipping out, and check that Jennie turns in her paper the next day?

These events occur suddenly, usually right when you are in the middle of teaching a lesson. If you stop more than momentarily, your class, which has an attention span measured in milliseconds rather than minutes, will become restless. For me, the easiest and quickest way to respond was to grab the pad of sticky notes that sat by my computer mouse pad, scribble a few terse words about what needed to be remembered, and then tear off the sheet and stick it on the border of my computer screen. Because I did attendance on the computer every hour, I was sure to see the note. Because most of these notes dealt with situations occurring in the next day or so, I would leave these notes on the screen until I made the call or solved the student issue.

Managing the Final Minutes of the Period

As the class period draws to a close, papers shuffle, notebooks close, and pens and pencils are stored as students anticipate their imminent escape to the halls. Meanwhile, you are trying to drive home those final critical points of the lesson, but you are fighting a losing battle. To refocus students on the lesson, walk over to the door while saying something like the following:

> *"I want to get this lesson done before the class period ends, but I don't think I'm going to make it, because it is hard for me to teach with all this extra activity going on. I am closing the door so that you will not be disturbed when students start passing in the hall."*

As you finish this statement, pull the door shut. Walking back to where you had been lecturing, you notice the room is dead quiet. Every eye is on you. You have their undivided attention. Nothing will hinder you as you wrap up the day's lesson. And nine times out of ten, you will finish before the bell rings, and your charges won't miss a second of passing time.

Another way of getting their cooperation is to phrase your words to show your concern for their welfare. How can students possibly find fault with your logic when you say, *"I am worried that you won't be able to finish,"* or *"I'm afraid that you won't know what to do on the assignment."* No matter what technique you use, once they figure out that their inattention could hinder their exit from the classroom, you will have them hanging on your every word.

As the minutes tick down to the end of the hour, the students become restless. But knowing they are desperate to leave works in your favor. Usually all you have to do is pause, and they, knowing you won't let them go until you're done, become quiet, attentive students again. Invariably someone will say, "Can we go yet?" or "Is it time to leave?" The first time this happens tell the students that you'll dismiss them when it's time and you would rather not be interrupted with queries about dismissal. The next time someone asks, respond by saying, *"I'll tell the rest of the class when they can leave, but you will need to stay after for a couple of minutes."* This response will end questions about when class is over.

> T I P Make sure that you establish a system for dismissing class. Most teachers give a hand signal or use a verbal cue, such as "You may leave now."

Sometimes students move to seats closer to the door at the end of the hour or even stand up and start toward the front of the room. This kind of behavior often happens when they think you are distracted and won't notice their surreptitious travel to the exit. To quash this behavior, announce that those who are in the wrong seat or who have moved to the front of the room when the bell rings will remain after class.

You can minimize problems at the end of class if the last part of your day's lesson engages the students' interest or is some type of activity. If you have some flexibility in the structure of your lesson, try to finish up with an exercise that the students will find stimulating.

Summary

Establishing classroom routines and developing classroom procedures help to channel adolescents' natural energy toward being productive rather than creating the ambiguities that lead to mischief. Over time, your classroom management skills will be honed to minimize student distractions. Think about the strategies presented in this chapter as you determine the best way to run your classroom.

- Before class begins, make sure that you have all the materials you need, check that the equipment you're using is operating properly, and know the lesson thoroughly.

- You can prevent many repetitive student questions by making sure you have students' attention before you give instructions, writing information on the board, distributing instructions on handouts, and posting key information in the classroom.

- From the first minutes of class to the last bell, you must work to keep students focused on the material you are teaching.

Conducting a Class Discussion

Much of the material presented in the preceding chapters deals with managing classroom behavior, which is a necessary first step to teaching. However, in time, as you become more effective with your discipline system, you'll be able to focus more on being a teacher and less on being a disciplinarian. That's why this chapter focuses on class discussions, which are a major part of teaching and education.

As a teacher, your goals in leading a class discussion are to

- Keep all students focused on the discussion
- Make students think about what is being discussed
- Help students learn and understand what is being discussed
- Get students to participate in the discussion
- Present an enjoyable and interesting lesson
- Not have to deal with behavior problems

This chapter presents several strategies to help you achieve these goals.

Preparing for a Discussion

Before class begins, try to have everything ready so that once you start the class discussion you won't have to break off to do other things. Although technology can be your friend, if it balks, your lesson may be sabotaged. So before you face your class, check and make sure your PowerPoint presentations and videos will perform exactly as planned and have a backup plan in mind. Be sure you have previewed all media. DVDs may not be what you think. Also, prepare any notes that you may want to provide in class.

When class begins, you have to prepare yourself and your students to participate in the discussion. This preparation includes positioning yourself in the room and telling students what your expectations are.

Providing Notes

If you're going to have notes on the board, put them up before starting the discussion. Turning your back to the class to write notes on the board is an invitation for the class to start acting up. If you want students to take notes only after the discussion is over, write the notes on the board before class and then pull a projector screen or rollup map down over them. The social studies teachers always have old maps, and your office secretary or custodian can usually supply you with clips for hanging the map. If you only want to expose a few notes at a time, write your first note on the bottom of the board, your next note above that, and so forth; put the last note at the top of the board. Then just raise the map, which had covered all the notes, a little at a time. It looks strange when the whole board is viewed, but it serves the purpose of giving students only a few notes at a time.

Another technique is to type up your notes using a very large font (24 point, for example) and then make transparencies that you can use on an overhead projector. Using a piece of paper, you can read one section or line at a time. This method saves you from rewriting notes on the board over and over.

Positioning Yourself in the Classroom

To lead a good discussion, you need to stand in front of the class and face the group. Just standing gives you an advantage over your seated students because you can see everyone's face. It is more difficult to be effective sitting at your desk. If your legs get tired, sitting on a stool will still put you high enough to see your students.

Although you may stand in one place for a while, walk around some. Students will wonder why you are moving and will tend to stay attentive. If a student is trying to write a note or converse with another student, she will stop doing that as you approach. By moving toward students who are misbehaving, you won't need to cut off the discussion or lecture to deal with the problem.

As you talk, make eye contact with all your students. This contact helps keep them focused on the lesson. As your gaze falls on a daydreaming student, you can almost see his mind snap back from wherever it might have been as the student suddenly thinks, "Ohmigosh, what's he saying? Is he going to ask me a question? I have to listen real close now and try to figure out what I've missed!" And if students are goofing off, pause the discussion and stare at them. They will hear the silence, look up to see you staring at them, and rejoin the lesson. You won't have to say a word to them.

Giving Your Expectations

Before starting the discussion, let the students know what kind of responses you expect. For example, when my students discussed literature, I told them that when they gave me an answer, I also wanted an explanation or reason why they chose that answer. In other words, I wanted them to be able to defend their answer.

To make sure that students are able to meet your expectations, you may want to consider having students prepare for the discussion. Giving questions a day ahead and having students write answers and bring them to class for the discussion forces the students to acquaint themselves with the lesson and give some thought to the topics being discussed. This kind of preparation also helps students who need more time to think about an answer to participate in class discussions.

Leading Discussions

When you ask a question, those students with answers raise their hands. The most efficient way to lead a discussion is to call on one of these students because you are guaranteed a response and a better-than-average chance of hearing a correct answer. This way may be the most efficient, but it is not the most effective way to lead a discussion. Because you rely on raised hands to get your answers, those students who don't raise their hands can tune you out. As long as their eyes are open, and their heads are up, they can safely daydream without being disturbed.

If your goal is to have a class discussion where all students have a decent chance to actually learn something, you will be doing more than just asking questions and calling on students who raise their hands. After all, the first kid with a hand up may not have the best answer or even a correct one. Sure, you will sometimes need to call on him in order to reward him for eager participation. However, keep in mind that not all students think at the same rate of speed. Some students need more time to put together their response. Therefore, after you have asked a question, especially one involving reasoning, wait before soliciting a response, because not all your students will instantly have an answer ready.

Even then don't just call on students with their hands up. If you start calling on students who don't have a hand raised, the anxiety level in the class will go up a bit, and all of your students will tend to pay better attention to what's going on. Also, don't follow a discernible pattern in your selection of respondents. Instead of calling on students row by row or alphabetically, pick your students randomly so no one will know when he or she will have to answer a question.

> **TIP** Several studies have shown that teachers, especially male ones, call on boys more often than girls. Periodically check to make sure you are not validating this study in the manner that you select student respondents.

Choosing Respondents

Using different formats for conducting class discussions helps make the process more interesting for you and your students. For a change, conduct a discussion but tell students that no one can raise his or her hand to supply an answer. You will just select people to respond. This tactic helps you to get new people responding to questions.

Another sure way to get some different voices heard in class discussions is to let the students choose who answers the question. You can do this in a couple of ways. Start by calling on someone to answer a question. If that student answers the question correctly, then she selects the next person to respond to a question. When a student gives a wrong answer or is stumped, I borrow an idea from the once-popular TV show "Who Wants to Be a Millionaire?" and ask him to call on a fellow student to be his "lifeline" and supply the right answer.

> **TIP** If a student's response is only partially correct, ask if someone wants to build on that answer or has more to add.

Another ploy to get more students participating involves taking a set of index cards and putting a student's name on each card. Drawing names from the deck keeps everyone attentive because all students have an equal chance of being called on to respond. Naturally after using a card you shuffle it back into the deck to create the possibility of that student being called on again.

If you are working from a list of questions that are written on the board or that students have before them, assign individual students specific questions. Then give them time to prepare their answers before you ask the question. To keep those without questions involved, tell the rest of the class that you will be randomly calling on them to produce information not given by the assignees or asking them to produce an additional or alternative answer.

To get 100 percent of your class focused on a single query, consider having all of the students write answers to a question you ask. This makes everyone a part of the discussion. While they are writing, walk around quickly spot-checking to see who wrote the correct answer and then select several students to read their answers.

Dealing with Students Who Want to Answer Every Question

Although senior high classes may be affected with acute apathy and instructors may find it hard to muster participation in discussions, such is rarely the case with junior high or middle school populations. These students love to talk, even if they have nothing to contribute. Often the same students are waving their hands, ready to yak about anything, and wanting to be called upon to answer every question. These kids may be the best students you have, or they may just like to talk. In either case, it can be annoying and distracting to see their hands shoot up every time you ask a question.

Talk privately with these students and explain to them that you appreciate their contributions to class discussions. However, point out that in order to be fair to the others in the class, you can't allow these students to dominate class discussions. Ask them whether it is okay with them if you call on them less frequently to contribute. This type of talk usually takes care of the problem.

Handling an "I Don't Know" Answer

Most of the time "I don't know" is an unacceptable answer because it's so easy to give. Too often kids give "I don't know" as an immediate automatic response to a question. No brainpower is needed for that reply. If you accept a rapid-fire "I don't know," it will become the response of choice for many students. Students need to know that in your class they have to attempt to answer questions.

When I received an "I don't know" answer, I rephrased the question, simplifying it, so that the student was faced with an easier question. If a student just couldn't come up with something, or I couldn't modify the original question, I told him I would be asking him another question in a few minutes. When I asked the second question, I made it an easier one so the student would be able to respond with an answer other than "I don't know."

If a student asked a question that I didn't know, I didn't fake an answer. Instead, if there seemed to be genuine interest in knowing the answer, I told the class that I would try to find out the answer and supply it the next day.

Occasionally you will be asked a question that is fairly basic, but its answer has slipped your mind. (Incidentally, this happens more frequently as you get older. Although older teachers' years of experience often give them the advantage in dealing with curriculum and classroom management situations, they're more apt to forget simple facts or even their students' names.) When this happens, you can either admit your lapse or call on the best student in the class to supply the information by asking him or her that same question. Hearing the student's answer, you will suddenly recall the lost information, and the class discussion can move forward again. (If you have forgotten a student's name, check your seating chart.)

Involving Students in the Discussion

You are in front of your students, and they are sitting there, the proverbial bumps on a log. Ask a question, and they just sit there staring back at you. It may be your students don't know the answer. In this case, shelve the discussion and shift back to a different teaching technique. However, sometimes you know they know the answer, and if it is not on the tip of their tongues, it's written on the homework sheets lying on the desks in front of them.

If they know the answer, why aren't they responding? Any, some, or all of the following reasons may be keeping their lips sealed:

1. They think that raising their hands with an answer is not cool because their peers will think they are sucking up to you.

2. They are not sure their responses are correct, and they will feel foolish if they are wrong.

3. They are afraid that their peers or you will ridicule their answers.

4. They don't understand the question or aren't sure what information you are seeking.

5. If they stall long enough, you will supply the answer, and they won't have to respond.

6. They believe that if they don't respond, the discussion will end, and the next class activity will be more enjoyable.

The first thing you can do to involve students in class discussions is to create a class environment where students feel comfortable sharing their ideas. You can start creating this environment beginning with your first teacher-student interaction of the school year. Make sure your demeanor is friendly. Remember this is a class discussion not an inquisition or cross-examination. The following sections explain other strategies for encouraging class participation.

Responding Positively to Incorrect Answers

Although you will naturally compliment students for offering good insights, you should also try to be positive when the responses miss the mark. Some examples of positive responses include the following:

"That's not exactly what I had in mind, but it is a good idea."

"You're close to being right."

"That's interesting."

"You're on the right track."

"I hadn't really thought of it in that way before."

"I can see how you might think that."

These responses all convey the message that although their answers aren't right, you value their insights. Terse answers such as "No, that's wrong," or other negative responses deflate egos fast. Negative responses quash not only that individual's desire to speak in class, but also discourage his classmates as well.

Using Discussions to Delay Assignments

Often your lesson plans indicate that when the discussion is over, you will begin a written assignment. Sharing this information with a class is the best way I know to stimulate discussion. Students faced with a choice between doing written exercises or having a class discussion invariably would rather raise their hands and start talking.

For example, my language arts class had been writing similes and metaphors. I had asked all of the students to create several to share in class. Adolescents, especially junior high age, don't like to read their creative efforts in class. Yet I needed to hear them so that the class could critique them and the students could improve on their next set of writing images. When I asked for volunteers, no hands went up. I began to get responses by calling on individuals, but some students declined to read their metaphors, and I decided not to force them. However, I needed to get more contributors, so I offered this observation:

> "We're going to stay with this topic all period. After you have written one simile or metaphor on the assigned topic, I'll invite everyone who wants to share his effort with the class to do so, and then I will assign you to write another one. So the more class participation we get, the longer it will take to critique your writings, and the less time will be spent writing additional similes and metaphors."

Once students realized that more time spent in discussion meant less time spent writing, almost everyone had metaphors to share.

The same gambit is just as effective when you are attempting to get students to discuss almost anything. I used it when I was trying to get them to elaborate on their analysis of literature. When I taught social studies, my students would put more effort into talking about current events and historical topics if they knew that after the discussion ended the class would be delving into another assignment.

Using Different Questions for Different Students

Most classes have a huge range of abilities. Teachers soon learn which students are Harvard material and which will need to apply themselves just to graduate from high school. By tailoring your questions to your students' abilities, you can make class discussions a challenging experience for all.

However, don't adhere rigidly to the premise of harder questions for the better students and easier questions for the less talented all the time. Not only will this practice become apparent to the students, but you also may have misjudged the students' abilities.

Shy students, often fearing failure, are reluctant to speak up in class. If you have a shy student, at the beginning of the year try to ask her questions that she can answer correctly so that she will be successful when she contributes in class.

Keeping the Discussion Lively

As you begin a class discussion, try to find a way to relate it to your students' interests or give them ideas on why the topic of discussion is relevant. Tell them why the topic is being discussed and what objectives you hope to accomplish.

Once you get started, stay on task. Try not to lose the momentum of the discussion by taking time for discipline. However, do what needs to be done to keep the class on task. If the class isn't attentive, pause, marker in hand, and write names on the board, if needed, until the class is quiet and ready to continue. If a student asks a question that is off topic, tell him that you will deal with it another time or that you would be willing to talk about it with him after class.

Being on task doesn't mean you should be straitlaced and boring. If you are entertaining, chances are your students will perk up and pay better attention. Try to inject humor or a little drama into the discussion. Show your interest in the subject. If possible don't just lecture or rely on the standard question-and-answer format, add some variety to the lesson. If you know an anecdote that can be quickly told and will catch your students' attention as well as enhance the lesson's objective, then tell it. Inject some role-playing into the activity or have a student come forward to demonstrate an idea. Sometimes I've had my classes chanting or echoing me. If your students are having fun, they're probably learning.

Don't let anyone drift away from the discussion. If a student is daydreaming, writing a note, or occupied in a social interaction, call him by name. Pause. Then ask the question. That will bring him back. If you ask the question first and then add his name, he will be slightly embarrassed because he probably did not hear the question. However, he is likely to start paying attention so that he will be ready if you call on him again. If your class is fading on you as you approach the end of the discussion, propose a game wherein the whole class wins a few minutes of free time as soon as five questions are answered correctly.

Summary

Verbal exchanges between teachers and students lie at the heart of the educational process. If you grab student interest with a topic, a sea of hands waved by eager respondents will appear. Like a band leader directing a performance with everyone on cue and in tune, skilled discussion leaders generate enthusiasm and compel student participation. Successful class discussions occur when teachers prepare adequately and know how to combine entertainment with instruction.

Keep the following points from this chapter in mind the next time you lead a class discussion:

- Stand and face your students when you ask questions. Maintaining eye contact and moving around the room during class discussions can help you keep the students' attention.

- Don't just call on students who raise their hands. Use different methods of choosing students to respond in order to engage the whole class in the discussion.

- You can make the discussion fun and interesting without letting the students get sidetracked from the topic you're teaching.

CHAPTER 16

Teaching in All Seasons

Ask someone to describe junior high students and you'll hear words like "enthusiastic," "energetic," "active," and "lively." Classroom life is never boring. If you need someone to run an errand to the office, a sea of hands wave wildly at you while a chorus of voices yell, "Can I go?" If you want a class discussion, just ask a question. Hands go up, and answers come forth. If they have anything at all to contribute, this age group will speak their minds. If there's going to be silence in a room, you must impose it. These students are excited and eager to do things. You had better have things under control, or you will have chaos. And this is just on regular schooldays. On holidays, special days, or whenever the weather changes, it gets even crazier.

Handling the Holidays

Recognize that holidays go beyond your classroom. If most staff members are dressing up for Halloween, passing out candy, and showing scary movies, you are going to be swimming against the current if you continue with business as usual. Sometimes you might want to wear something appropriate to the occasion or even tailor a lesson to follow a holiday theme. Even so, most teachers are relieved when Valentine's Day, St. Patrick's Day, April Fool's Day, or Halloween fall on a weekend.

Valentine's Day

The girls love Valentine's Day (February 14). The guys enjoy the candy hearts and the chocolate strictly for their culinary value. They don't do cards. The girls, however, put tremendous energy into writing, giving, and reading Valentine cards and letters. Because Valentine's Day is a sugar holiday, the end of the day doesn't come fast enough for most teachers. I'm not sure whether sugar makes kids hyper, but I am certain the social nature of passing it around and eating it excites kids.

St. Patrick's Day

Wear green on St. Patrick's Day (March 17), no matter what your heritage. To show up without something green on will get you heckled and maybe pinched. Yes, pinched. Some years students will pinch anyone not wearing green. Other years, if no one starts the pinching thing, St. Pat's Day comes and goes without getting much attention. Enjoy those years.

April Fool's Day

Be vigilant on April Fool's Day (April 1). It's a good day to stay close to your classroom. If you stray away, your students may rearrange your room, hide your stuff, and wreak all kinds of havoc. Be suspicious of whatever students say to you. They will report the untimely death of a student, tell you that you have been called to the office, and even wear bandages and casts trying to convince you that they have been injured. If you are a guy, check your fly, because you can expect to hear them say all day, "Mr. Foley, your fly is down," and you want to be sure. Just keep your guard and your fly up.

Halloween

Really Halloween is a three-day holiday. First it's Devil's Night (October 30), which is when pranks are pulled. Then it's Halloween

(October 31), and on November 1 all the kids are pretty well gorged on sweets and carrying a supply with them. This definitely is not the time to bring forth your most challenging work.

For a while, my school had problems with students soaping school windows and throwing trash at the school on Devil's Night and Halloween. I used to close the door during each class, swear my students to secrecy, and warn them that police officers and staff would be watching the building on those nights and videotaping pranksters. I told the students that I wasn't supposed to tell them about the video-taping, but I didn't want my students getting in trouble, so I was leaking this information. There wasn't anyone even watching the buildings on those nights, but I figured if the students thought there was someone there, they would stay away. Maybe my words reached the right people, but for whatever reason, once I started leaking information, the soaping and trashing ended.

For years the building I taught in housed grades six, seven, and eight. Students and staff dressed in costume during the afternoon of Halloween. I would bring a lantern, turn off the lights, and read Edgar Allen Poe stories to my class by lamplight. I felt I was observing the spirit of the holiday without totally wasting the day.

Then the sixth and seventh grades left, and the school became an eighth and ninth grade building. The costumes were replaced by dyed hair in shades of green, pink, or blue and exotic makeup. Because there was no dress code ruling on hair or makeup, the teachers let it go. I usually spent a couple of days with Poe, reading and interpreting the poem "The Raven" and the short story "The Telltale Heart." It fit with the language arts curriculum and seemed appropriate for Halloween.

> **T I P** Halloween and all the holidays are good times to build friendships with your students as you joke with them and compliment them on their makeup and hairstyles.

Candy is everywhere the day after Halloween. Consider allowing students to eat it on that day only, but not once class starts. If they try eating candy during class, confiscate their candy until after school and make the candy eaters pick all the wrappers off the floor after class.

The Christmas Season

Although you can totally miss holidays like Valentine's Day, Halloween, or April Fool's Day if they fall on a weekend, the Christmas season is unavoidable. Students are busier than Santa's elves as Christmas approaches. Holiday choir performances, band concerts, the winter dance, decorations in the rooms and halls, and all the frenzied Christmas commercialism do not go undetected by students. Their energy, a combination of exuberance and anxiety, is unmistakable.

Although you might like to, you can't quit teaching during the last two weeks before winter break. The best strategy I found was to back off from heavier, more taxing stuff such as essay writing and literature analysis and go for lighter stuff like reading poetry or a play. One year I had students write a Christmas story with a moral; that assignment was well received.

Keep in mind also that this can be a stressful time for students, as both the anxiety and anticipation of the holidays may accentuate student behaviors. Expect students to be more excitable, sometimes even giddy, but be aware that students whose home environment is unhappy may be more withdrawn or aggressive in school during this time.

Dealing with a Bad Day

Some days you just don't feel like teaching. You could be sick, beset with problems, worn out, or just feeling lethargic. In any event, knowing you'll be facing five or six groups of students starts to feel like a seven-hour marathon. Unless you are blessed with classes of juniors and seniors where you might just be able to have them catch up on past work or start a reading assignment, you can bet your classes won't take mercy on you and be angelic. Sitting at your desk all day while the students work quietly at their seats is probably not going to happen with a room full of middle school or junior high students. No, when you least want to teach is when you have to be most prepared.

If you had planned a tough teaching day of lecturing, leading discussion, or monitoring small groups at work, you might see whether you can modify your plan so you won't have to directly interact with the class most of the period. Nevertheless, make sure whatever lesson you assign is one that will keep students occupied and relates to what you've been doing. If the assignment is boring or obviously busywork, you'll likely encounter more discipline problems than usual.

You may gain more cooperation if you're honest with them. Telling your students that you're not feeling well or that you're having a bad day may elicit some sympathy. But this will happen only if you have good rapport with your students.

If you're not feeling well, you might say something like this:

"I'm not feeling well today, so it's a little harder for me to teach. I'm not going to be able spend a lot of time settling down the class and dealing with behavior problems, so I hope you'll be cooperative because instead of issuing warnings, I'll just write names on the board."

At this point, pick up the marker and begin teaching. At the first disturbance, write a name on the board. Your students will see you mean business and will become quite cooperative.

Even though you may not be feeling well or may feel frustrated, don't take it out on your students. Realize that your problems were there before class started and it's not fair to make them suffer.

Coping with Tragedy

Traumatic events such as the death of a student or faculty member, as well as major occurrences such as the terrorist destruction of the

World Trade Center so transfix your students that teaching becomes impossible. Suddenly you are dealing with a problem that falls well beyond the scope of your curriculum. Your education methods and child psychology teacher education courses don't tell you what to do with a class full of grief-stricken students or a class who has just watched an airplane crash into a building on television.

In the immediate aftermath of student-related tragedy, students are too upset and distraught to deal with that day's academic plan. They need a chance to talk, and they often look to the teacher for help. Under these circumstances, your best option is to let the students express themselves. To keep some measure of control, insist that the students raise their hands and let only one student talk at a time. If you feel comfortable doing so, talk and offer advice, saying things that will help the students accept or understand the situation. Most teachers have lived long enough to have had the experience of dealing with the death of a loved one or close friend. For students this might be the first time.

These class discussions are also helpful for those students who might not have known the deceased. From hearing classmates talk, they will learn about the tragedy and gain some understanding about the circumstances of the death or information about the student.

Do you devote the whole class period to this type of discussion? This might happen, but more than likely there will come a point when you sense that the issue has been covered and that those students who felt that they had to talk have done so. At this juncture, it is time to ease into the planned lesson. Students who are especially distraught can be given a pass to see the counselor.

Most school districts have a plan for dealing with tragic events. When such a happening occurs, they may bring in counselors from around the district, implement crisis committees, or initiate other plans of action, because they realize a sudden tragedy can have a dramatic effect on students and staff.

I was teaching in the classroom the day the Challenger spacecraft blew up and the day that the World Trade Center was destroyed. When these devastating images appeared on the television, all of us were shocked. Surprisingly, the students didn't seem to know how to react or what to think. Most were totally out of touch with current events. The exploding images on the TV screen looked more like scenes from a disaster movie to them than news stories.

Being the only adults present as these events unfolded, teachers were the ones that the students turned to for an explanation. Many of us on the staff used our class periods to try and put some historical perspective on these events by supplying information on the space program and terrorism. This probably is the best way to deal with spectacular news events. For at that moment, teachers are in the enviable position of dealing with students who suddenly are vitally interested in learning all they can about the news story that they are witnessing. If you can supply objective, unbiased information at this time, you may have taught them a lesson that they will never forget.

Changing Weather and Changing Seasons

Winter is a big deal in Cadillac, the community in northern Michigan where I taught. Winter means skiing, snowmobiling, sledding, and ice fishing. As autumn fades into cold, gray November, students (and some teachers) are all watching for that first snow. When the first flurry of snowflakes blows by the window, everyone's energized. Academically, they're dumbstruck. You can't beat Mother Nature, so I just let them cram around the windows and look for a couple of minutes. Then the class returns to the lesson. But I realize that the only thing filling their brain that hour is snow.

One day you are freezing, and the next day the sun's shining, the snow piles are shrinking, and suddenly you and all your students would rather be doing anything but concentrating on the day's lesson. Unfortunately you probably have four to six weeks of school left. At least that's what happens if you are living in most states north of the Mason-Dixon Line. Unlike the holiday madness that comes and goes in a day or two, spring fever lingers.

The warm days soon become hot ones, and in buildings that aren't air-conditioned, you feel like you are teaching in a sauna. Nevertheless, you can't fold the academic tent and go to a steady diet of word searches and videos. No matter what the weather is doing, you have to keep your students focused on learning. The following sections provide ideas to help you pull students' attention away from the weather outside and back to the classroom.

Snow Days

If students are in school on a day when the weatherman and the Doppler radar are forecasting a winter storm, the words *snow day* are on everyone's lips, and the "if when" questions start coming. "If we get a snow day, when will this be due?" Once the forecast of heavy snow is made, students become gamblers. Whatever homework is assigned, their efforts to complete it are tempered with the odds of a snow day.

Students and teachers in northern Michigan (where I taught) can expect three to five snow days each winter. Students like to assume that when ice and snow wipes out the school day, their assignment due dates are postponed. With a short-term project that is being worked on in class, invariably the due date is moved. However, with long-term assignments that are not being worked on in class, the original date stays firm. If the weather calamity occurs on the due date, the work is due the first day students return to school. With storms in the forecast, I remind students to take their work home with them so that they can work on it at home if they are snowed in.

You must be very clear to students that the homework is due the next day that they are in class, whether it is tomorrow or the day after. Say this to them twice. Write it on the board. Make sure it's the last thing they hear when they leave the room. Cross your fingers. Hope for the best, but expect the worst. Woodland animals hunker down during winter storms and go dormant. Students reach a similar level of academic inactivity.

Students and teachers scrutinize winter weather forecasts with the eagerness that Wall Street brokers follow their stocks. To have a snow day declared causes instant celebration among the total school population. However, on those wintry days when your school is in session while neighboring districts' buildings are closed, the mood becomes ugly. If you think it's tough to motivate students on a normal day, wait until your school is the only one in session on a stormy day.

On these days, I would usually note that it was a tough call for school administrators to make when they were out in the wee hours of the morning driving around trying to predict what the weather would be like when school started. I would also point out that when students got an unexpected day of vacation, many households had to scramble to find childcare. But I also confided to them that teachers were just as eager to be out on a snow day.

Because the entire class was disappointed about being in school on such a snowy day, I would give students 30 seconds to moan and whine about the situation. For the next half-minute, students would rant, complain, and voice their displeasure, and I would join them in this disruption. Then I would quiet the class, say that we were going to make the best of it, and begin to teach the planned lesson. I found that this technique allowed them to blow off steam, and once that was done, the day went well.

Falling Barometers and Full Moons

When a teacher claims that classroom behavior degenerates as the barometer falls or during a full moon cycle, those who aren't teachers may scoff. But they haven't tried to keep students on task when the sky fills with thunderheads. Similarly if a teacher struggles all day to maintain control, even with classes that are normally cooperative, a check with a lunar chart is apt to show that it's the time for a new or full moon.

Rather than struggling alone with student behavior during these times, I have found peer pressure to be an ally. To make this happen, I tell the class the following story:

> *"Have you ever noticed how when a storm is coming that the birds start making a racket, or maybe your pet dog starts running around or barking? If you have younger brothers or sisters, they probably get hyper or really noisy. Do you all know that just before a rainstorm or during a full moon, the fish bite? This all happens because during certain phases of the moon or when the barometer is falling, animals, birds, fish, and even humans who are less well-developed emotionally or are less mature can't help but react. They really can't help it. In a class like this, you can even see this effect. Those who are mature continue to behave well because the changes in nature have no effect on them. Those who aren't as mature emotionally fidget, speak out, and in general have trouble with self-control. On a day like today, as we carry on with class activities, watch and you can see by students' behavior who is unable to settle down. Don't be angry with these people, because they can't help it. When they become a little more mature, they will be able to handle these changes better."*

After I tell that story, behavior usually improves, because I have alerted the whole class that those who misbehave can't really help it because they are immature. To act out under these circumstances is to be seen as being immature by your peers, and no kid wants to be seen in that light.

Spring Fever

You can use the onset of pleasant weather to motivate students by offering the option of holding class outside on nice days. To get outside, however, students have to earn the privilege by meeting some expectations. The choices here depend on the nature of your classes and the curriculum. A class with some discipline problems can earn a class period outside as a reward for several class periods of good behavior. If a class has a major assignment, their escape outside can depend on getting a certain percentage of papers turned in. Whatever you decide, be very specific on the standards to be met and make sure the classes know exactly what they have to accomplish to earn a class period outside. In setting standards, select standards that are slightly better than the norm, but not unreasonably high. It helps if you act like you really want to go out and sure hope they behave and meet the qualifying standard needed to escape the building.

> T I P Check with your administration before you introduce the idea of going outside to your classes. Some school administrations forbid taking students out or have special instructions you should know.

Once a group qualifies to go outside, point out that they can't go unless certain weather conditions are met. For example, from past experience I learned that the ground must be dry, because the class would be sitting on it. The air temperature has to be at least 60, and the winds have to be light. Any less favorable conditions will leave you trying to teach in front of shivering students or those who won't sit on the ground.

If the class meets the standard and the weather cooperates, you can head outside. As you leave the building, put a note on the classroom door telling where the class is going. Also, notify the office that the class will be outside. Once the class is outside, tell the students that you actually will be conducting class. It will not be a social hour or a chance to catch a nap. Point out that if anyone needs to go inside, everyone has to go inside because students aren't allowed to wander the building alone. Also, indicate that the third time that you have to ask individuals or the group to behave, everyone will go in. This statement creates peer pressure to behave because the actions of a few could jeopardize the experience for the whole group.

Conducting a class outside works best in situations when the students are doing a reading assignment, you are giving a basic lecture not needing visual aids, or everyone is working in small groups. Having a class do writing assignments would be difficult. These ventures can be fun, although you must be strict once the students are outside and take them back in early if they don't behave according to the criteria you have established.

If going outside isn't appealing, you can sometimes offer the chance to visit a more comfortable environment. The building where I taught was not air-conditioned. If it was 80 outside, it was liable to be at least 80 degrees in my room. However, the school had air-conditioned classrooms in the back of the auditorium. In exchange for good classroom behavior, I would take classes to the auditorium and do classwork there.

Summary

Holidays, tragedies, and spring fever happen. You can't blithely ignore these occurrences and teach on, oblivious to them. On the other hand, if you shut down your program for every special occasion, you will never cover your curriculum. It's best to compromise. Acknowledge the event by perhaps easing back on your lesson plan or adapting your teaching to the holiday. Keep in mind the ideas presented in this chapter.

- Although you can make some allowances for the holidays, do your best to keep students focused on learning. Limit the candy and other treats and watch out for pranks and other misbehavior.

- When a tragedy occurs, give students a chance to express their feelings about the event. Offer the class your thoughts and perspective on the event as well.

- Make sure students know that they must still meet deadlines even when school is cancelled because of bad weather. When the weather is good, you can use a class period outside as an incentive for good behavior or improved academic performance.

CHAPTER 17

Working with Parents

Typically there is a direct link between parental expectations and a student's educational plan. If an *A* will earn a student a chance to go to summer basketball camp, then *As* are the goal. If *Cs* are needed to continue to use the Internet or play video games, then that becomes the goal. Every new teacher soon learns that this is how the system works. To be most effective, teachers need parental support. This chapter provides insight on how best to communicate with parents in order to help their children succeed in school.

The Parent-Teacher Conference

Most nonteaching adults would be highly anxious, if not petrified, at having to face a roomful of middle school or junior high students. However, for some teachers the students are the easy part. It's talking to the parents that's scary. Typically, you have about 15 minutes per parent-teacher conference, and you may have anywhere from just a few to perhaps 40 earnest folks wanting to hear about their child. The following sections provide ideas to help you make the most of this meeting.

Planning for Parent-Teacher Conferences

Conducting successful conferences becomes more likely if you have done some planning. If your school district schedules parents or parents call ahead and make appointments, pre-conference preparation is fairly easy. If conferences are "drop-ins" wherein any parent can come at any time, your preparations will be less precise. With this situation, have all student portfolios close by so you can quickly find records and information for parents.

Before conferences start, try to have these items handy:

- A portfolio of the student's work
- An up-to-date calculation of the student's grades
- Documentation concerning behavior problems
- A class syllabus
- A seating chart
- Copies of tests and assignments
- Information about long-range homework assignments or class projects
- Copies of textbooks and materials used in class

Having this stuff at hand saves you having to rummage around in a file drawer or dig through shelves with a parent sitting in front of you. You can quickly answer questions about what is being taught in your class and where the student sits and who sits near them. In addition, giving parents a copy of assignment information helps them make sure their child turns the work in on time. If the student is missing assignments, you can give these to the parents to pass on to their child.

Conducting the Parent-Teacher Conference

Now that you have your materials handy, what are you going to say to these parents? First, if possible, meet the parents at the door of your classroom and greet them by name. Either sit with them on chairs or have them sit adjacent to you at your desk. Try not to have a barrier, such as your desk, between you and the parents. Plan on showing parents their child's grades and papers found in their portfolios and discussing with them any academic difficulties that the child may be experiencing. If there are behavior problems, tactfully discuss your concerns. (See the section in this chapter on "The Phone Call Home" for more specifics.)

Sometimes if the child is well behaved and earns good grades, everything pertinent can be said in about 2 minutes. However, most parents feel that a conference should last at least 10 minutes. After you have told the parents the information they need to know regarding grades and any behavior problems, try to get them talking. They may have concerns or thoughts that will enable you to be more effective in working with their child. Being a good listener is key to conducting good parent-teacher conferences.

Here are some questions to ask or statements to make that may stimulate further conversation:

> *"Do you have any questions or concerns about this class?"*

> *"Has your daughter talked about this class?"*

> *"Let me show you what kind of work that we are doing ..."* (At this point, you could discuss the class syllabus, show them textbooks, explain how you grade, or give them examples of homework assignments or tests.)

> *"How is your son enjoying this year in the junior high?"*

Once you've completed the necessary discussion about your class, feel free to comment about that child's extracurricular activities. A statement such as, *"Your daughter seems to enjoy playing on the basketball team,"* or *"Jim showed me the medal he won at the solo ensemble music festival,"* are good conversation starters. At the end of the conference, summarize your main points and reiterate information received from the parent that you need to take action on. End on a positive note.

The parent-teacher conference is your chance to show that you like teaching, enjoy kids, and are happy to have their child in your class. When that happens, parents leave the conference confident that you are doing a good job as their child's teacher.

Providing Perspective

Parent-teacher conferences, although generally thought of as opportunities to discuss academic and socialization issues, may offer you the opportunity to help parents get a realistic appraisal of their children. Parents may know more than you do about their child, but you know more about adolescents in general than parents do. Dealing with classrooms filled with adolescents year after year makes you an expert in adolescent behavior. Over time you will gain insights and an understanding about the nature of adolescents that goes far beyond that of most parents.

Parents, on the other hand, acquire their knowledge about adolescents from raising their own and having contact with their children's friends. With this limited exposure to adolescents, parents may believe that all adolescents behave similarly to their children or may think that their child is the only one in the world who behaves a certain way. You may be able to give these parents a better perspective about their child.

When parents talk about their experiences with their child, they may be looking to you for ideas to improve the situation. Parents may make statements such as, "He has no interest in schoolwork. All he does is watch television and play video games," or "She doesn't talk to us anymore. She only talks to her girlfriends." Other parents complain that their children don't listen to them or are disrespectful. Parents whose child last year was thrilled to do things with them now find their child no longer wants to be seen with them. Things like this make parents wonder if something is wrong with them.

As a teacher, you know this behavior is typical for adolescents, but to a parent it is baffling. They wonder whether their child is normal and whether they are being good parents. Taking a few minutes to assure distraught parents that their child is normal can be helpful. Go on to explain that as a teacher who gets to know more than a hundred students each year, you have learned that adolescence is the point in life where many kids begin to assert their independence and seek to strengthen relationships with peers rather than parents. Don't preach to these adults, yet if they seem interested and eager for any help that anyone can offer them, give them some ideas on how they might improve their relationship with their child.

Dealing with Angry Parents

You will rarely find yourself facing angry parents. This situation might occur only once every 5 or 10 years. When the situation happens, stay calm and listen. These people clearly have information they want you to hear, so you had better listen. Don't interrupt them unless it is to ask for clarification. Empathize with them and try to see the issue from their perspective. Be willing to admit it if you have made mistakes; however, don't let them berate you.

Angry parents aren't always good listeners. As you talk with them, keep these tips in mind:

- Speak slowly and realize that you may have to repeat your points or explain them in several ways.

- Be careful of what you say. You don't want to be misinterpreted.

- Do not get emotional or angry and don't raise your voice.

If the parents won't settle down and the conference is going nowhere, suggest asking an administrator to join the conference.

> TIP   If you have a feeling that an upcoming conference will be difficult, let the administrator know ahead of time. He or she then can be sure to be available if needed.

The Student-Led Conference

In the traditional parent-teacher conference, the teacher talks about the child, shows his work, discusses his assets and shortcomings while the parent listens, adds observations, and then both parties decide what the child will or won't be doing during the rest of the year. It sometimes can be almost like a trial. Evidence is presented, testimony is given, perhaps a little cross-examination occurs, and then a verdict is rendered. Except that in a court case, the defendant is able to tell his side of the story.

With the student-led conference (SLC), the student is more than just a participant, he's the lead player. With an SLC, everyone hears everything that is said, and there is the opportunity for all versions of a story to be heard. Ideally in an SLC, the student does most of the talking, and the parents direct questions to their child instead of the teacher.

The SLC is not a perfect vehicle for a parent-teacher conference. The teacher and parent aren't going to be able to share information that they don't want the child to hear unless they banish the child to the hall. To do this is not only awkward but is also liable to plant a little paranoia in the child's mind. He will find himself wondering as he stands in the hall, "Just what have I done that they can't talk about it in front of me?" and "What dark secrets do they have that they don't want me to know about?"

Student-led conferences can also be unpleasant when parents make a show for the teacher of dressing down the child and telling him exactly how things will be for him when they get home. The atmosphere can also be distressing for the student when it appears like his parents and his teacher are ganging up on him.

However, the conference will be a success if the teacher and student do the necessary preparation, and all parties remember that, as its name suggests, it is a conference led by a student. With the student, the parents, and the teacher present, a true picture of the school situation can be rendered.

Preparing Students for an SLC

The preparation for a student-led conference starts the first week of school when the teacher tells the students that they will be keeping their work in portfolios and will be sharing this work with their parents at conference time. As the teacher continues to elaborate on the process, the students realize that if they have little or nothing in the folder when the conference occurs, there will be 15 minutes of dead air. The student will have a hard time keeping the conference on a positive note with everyone staring into an empty folder.

Having a portfolio of *D* work is only marginally better than having nothing, so suddenly there's incentive to put some effort into what goes in the portfolio. The teacher usually dictates that key assignments must be included in the portfolio, but these can be redone if the student is not satisfied with the final product. The student can select the rest of the portfolio's contents.

To help students prepare for the conference, have them fill out the Student Conference Assessment Sheet (included in this chapter for your reference), which asks them to discuss the things they do well, areas that need improvement, what they are most proud of, and their goals. You will need a class period or two to work with these sheets because most students aren't used to doing self-evaluation tasks. During these sessions, use sample work to show how to spot the strengths and weaknesses of an assignment. This process is quite similar to peer editing done in writing classes or what an instructor does in grading student work. It is time well spent, because most students really have no idea how to critique their work. Those students who pick up on this skill often show improvement with their assignments.

Scheduling the SLC

Student-led conferences can be made mandatory or offered as an option to the traditional parent-teacher conference. Some school districts have a 30-minute conference period with the first half of the conference being an SLC. Others use an SLC format, but at the end of the conference the student leaves so the teacher and parents can talk privately.

Student Conference Assessment Sheet

These are things I want you to notice about my work:

1. _____
   _____

2. _____
   _____

3. _____
   _____

I believe these are things I do well:

1. _____
   _____

2. _____
   _____

3. _____

My favorite piece of work is _____

I think my work could be better if I_____

_____

_____

_____

_____

My goal for next term is _____

_____

_____

> **TIP** Topics such as teaching methods, the child's relationships with other students, and how the child compares to others in the class should be discussed without the child present.

Although the goal is to have the student conduct the entire conference, teachers may want to ease into the process by having the student lead a portion of the conference and then having the teacher conduct a portion. The teacher then has the opportunity to discuss goals and objectives for the class or give general information about the curriculum.

Helping Parents Appreciate SLCs

Because SLCs represent a dramatic break from the traditional parent-teacher conference, parents may be skeptical. You are likely to have parents make it clear to you that they can talk to their child anytime about schoolwork, but the conference is the only time they can consult with a teacher. Other parents may be uncomfortable talking to their child about schoolwork. If parents are adamant about these issues, you may have to meet with them without the child being present.

To switch from the traditional parent-teacher conference to the SLC format involves salesmanship as you emphasize the positives that result from having a student showing and discussing his work while talking about his school experience. Most staff, after working with both types of conferences, prefer to use the SLC for most of their face-to-face meetings with parents.

The Phone Call Home

If a student is doing poorly in your class, just sending a progress report home may not be enough, because there is no guarantee that the parents will see the progress report. A parent phone call or conference is the best way to bring about a change, whether the problem is with student behavior or scholastic performance.

First, try to reach the parent at home. This may be difficult because parents may be working during the hours you are calling. Trying calls during your conference hour, right after school, and in the evening, however, will usually connect you with a parent. If you can't reach parents at home, try calling the parent's job site. When you can't reach a parent by telephone, send your information through the mail.

Parent phone calls seem to fall into one of these categories:

"Your child is really doing well."

"Your child is doing poorly academically."

"Your child is misbehaving."

If a student is not turning in his assignments, then a call home is needed. However, before you pick up the phone, inform the student of your intentions. Typically, I would call the student up to my desk and have a conversation something like the following:

Me: *"Billy, I haven't received the book summary that was due last week. I feel it's time I called home so that your parents can be aware of this problem. I can't call tonight, but give me your phone number so I can stick it right next to my computer monitor so that I'll remember to make the call tomorrow."*

Billy: "Will you call my parents if I turn in my book summary tomorrow in class?"

Me: *"I guess I won't need to call if you have done a good job on it and I get it tomorrow."*

The odds were pretty good that I would have Billy's book summary the next day. Otherwise, I would make the call.

This technique also works well when the problem is misbehavior. You just ask for the phone number and inform the student that the next time there is a problem you will call his parents. In some cases, this warning will cause a sudden positive change of attitude, and you will realize that you have found your magic bullet. But if the threat of a call doesn't deter the student and the problem starts up again, make the call.

Rarely do you really need to ask a student for his phone number because you can find the number readily in the student directory or in the student information on file in the office. However, when you personally ask a student for the number, he suddenly realizes that home contact is imminent, and in most cases he will make a sudden effort to get work in or change his behavior in order to prevent parent contact.

The Phone Call About Low Grades

"Mrs. Smith, I'm Dave Foley, your son's language arts teacher, and I'm concerned about Kenton's work in my class. I was hoping that we could work together to help him improve his performance in language arts."

I usually opened my phone conversations with parents with a comment like that. I wanted parents to know that I was concerned and that by working as a team we could help their child. I would then give specifics on what the problem was. Most of the time, it was assignments that were poorly done or not done at all. I then waited to hear what the parents' reactions were.

Parent responses have a huge range. At one end are those parents who are very involved with their child and aware that there is a problem with their child's classroom performance. Typically they are monitoring and helping with homework and are using a system of incentives, both negative and positive, to motivate the child to improve.

At the other end of the spectrum are the parents who seem at a loss when it comes to providing home support. Some parents are never home, often because their work schedule prevents them from seeing their child during after-school hours. Others will make statements such as, "All my child does is watch television. He never does his homework," or "He always tells me he has all his homework done."

In my school system, students who failed two subjects had to make up the work in summer school or repeat the grade. In a nice way, I made parents aware of this fact and subtly suggested that they might have to curtail some privileges until their child's grade improves. By limiting Internet surfing, television watching, telephone use, or the opportunities to be with friends until the grade reaches a C, the parents could give their child an incentive to work harder in class. On the other hand, offering a reward such as money for a movie or CD if the grade improved might motivate the child to work in my class. I emphasized that they knew their child best and could probably determine what would work.

I used to hesitate to suggest specific parent intervention plans. However, I found a surprising number of parents who never thought about removing privileges or offering rewards as a means of changing academic performance. Often these parents seemed genuinely happy to learn a technique for motivating their children to work in school.

In my phone conversations, I usually asked if there was something happening in class that might be making it difficult for their child to succeed. Over the years I learned in parent phone conversations about students who couldn't see the board because they wouldn't wear their glasses and students who were being bullied. I was glad to learn these things.

In every conversation with parents, try to say something positive. Make a comment such as, *"I know Jimmie is not always as dedicated to his homework as he should be, but he is well behaved and a good citizen, and I enjoy having him in class."* If the kid is hyperactive and a discipline problem as well, still try to be positive by saying, *"Although sometimes it's a little more than I need, I appreciate Jimmie's enthusiasm and eagerness to participate in class activities."*

The Phone Call for Misbehavior

When talking to parents, tell them you are concerned because their child's behavior is interfering with his learning and also making it difficult for his classmates to learn. Point out that the measures you have been using (reprimands, minutes after class, seat changes) haven't worked, and you are afraid you may have to resort to detentions or trips to the office.

The parents may suddenly realize that their lives are about to be inconvenienced as they will get calls from the office and have to make special transportation arrangements for their child to be picked up after detention. Ask them if they have any ideas on how you might be more successful with their child. Then listen. Oftentimes, they'll volunteer to take the issue up with their child. The conversation usually ends here 99 percent of the time. The child's behavior either shows sudden improvement, or you realize that you will have to solve the problem without parental assistance. In any event, you have also given notice to the parent that

- There is a problem
- This problem may encroach upon the parents' lives

When the child is punished, the parents can't say they weren't warned.

> T I P Make a note of the date you made the call to the parents in case the parents claim they didn't hear from you.

The 1 percent of the time a call is unpleasant is when parents become hostile. Appease them if you can. If they are unreasonable, politely say, "Good night," and hang up. This situation happened to me only twice in 30 years.

The Phone Call from a Child to His Parent

Having a child call his parents and then tell them personally about misbehavior he has just committed can be an effective deterrent to future misbehavior. When the child confesses his classroom crime over the phone, the parent has little recourse but to side with you.

Sometimes you end up just sitting there while the parent chews out the child or metes out punishment over the phone. By the time the parent is done, any further punishment on your part isn't necessary.

The situation becomes a little more challenging when the child opens the conversation with the parent by saying, "Mr. Foley is making me call you, but I didn't do nothing." You will probably hardly notice the grammatical error of saying "nothing" instead of "anything" as you mentally start to develop your defense. When the phone receiver ends up in your hand, as it will almost as soon as the student makes his not guilty plea, listen for any comment by the parent and then calmly recall the events that prompted the call. Use the strategies referred to in the section on "The Phone Call for Misbehavior." Most of the time the parent winds up supporting you.

> T I P Never make a student call home unless you are absolutely sure the student is the culprit and the problem merits the parent's attention.

A word of caution: Do not make a student call his parents if you are the only adult in a room full of students. Even though it may help curtail other students' impulse to misbehave if they see one of their peers having to call his parents, don't make the call. In the first place, while you are dealing with the call, no one is monitoring your class's behavior or continuing the lesson. Secondly, there is no way you can be sure how long the call will take or what the reaction of the parent will be. You could be tied up for a long time and/or have to deal with an angry parent. Neither of these situations should occur with your students present.

Parents, Teachers, and Planners

Any information you can send home about your class will be appreciated. By providing material on your classroom policies, you have forewarned parents. If problems occur and you must contact them about their child's misbehavior, it's hard for them to be shocked if they have received information about your class earlier in the year.

Putting a copy of the due dates of long-range assignments in the hands of parents helped my students to meet their deadlines. This copy was called the "refrigerator copy" in hopes that it would be attached to refrigerator doors in my students' homes. In addition, I provided a second sheet telling the correct procedure for writing a book summary so that parents would know what I required.

When students can't be relied upon to complete their work on time, the parents and the teacher need to team up to get the student on track academically. In this situation, the parents need to know what's going on in class in order to make sure the student keeps his work up-to-date, so teachers send assignment due dates home either through e-mail or written communication carried home with the child.

However, students aren't as resolute about their mission as the pony express. Memos from school typically are delivered to parents about as frequently as cats obey their owner's commands. The only way to guarantee that messages are successfully carried back and forth between parents and teachers involves using negative reinforcement for noncompliance. In other words, if the child fails to deliver the message in a timely fashion, the parent disciplines the child.

Giving the child a planner or notebook, which he presents to the teacher once a week, seems the best way to allow parents and teachers to stay in contact. In the planner, the teacher writes upcoming assignments and details progress or the lack thereof from the previous week's work. However, it is the child's responsibility to give the planner to the teacher each week. Parents should not expect the teacher to ask specifically for the planner each Friday. If they do and the teacher fails to ask for the planner, the child (and sometimes the parent) may blame the teacher for his failure to turn in his work.

When a Parent Does a Student's Work

When I suspected a parent might have done one of my eighth grade language arts student's writing compositions, I hesitated to make an accusation, because occasionally I would have a student who actually did his or her best work outside the classroom. Still, if the homework was significantly better than the work in class, I suspected that there might be a ghostwriter.

In a conference with the student, I would compare his in-class efforts with his homework, pointing out how much better he seemed to be able to work outside class. I would note how important it was for him to do his own work and indicate that although some proofreading help from home was fine, the student must generate his own original ideas and express them in his own writing style.

To help him produce the same quality of work in class, I would ask if there was anything I could do to help him. Sometimes he would ask about a seating change or additional work time, and if feasible, I would accommodate him.

I followed up with a phone call telling the parent about the discrepancy between her child's homework and in-school assignments without accusing her of ghostwriting. I pointed out that as the child moves into high school, he would need to be able to produce quality work in the classroom as he encountered more essay questions, state-mandated writing tests, and compositions. I then would ask the parent for suggestions for improving her child's in-class performance.

Addressing the problem in this way is good public relations, and you occasionally can obtain some helpful information when you ask the parent for her ideas on how the situation might be improved. In the days following this parent contact, there usually will be a change. Oftentimes future homework assignments, while still good, will begin to show signs that the parent is helping the child to improve his work instead of doing the work for him.

Summary

Keep these points in mind as you convey needed information to parents about their child's academic progress and, if there are any, behavior concerns:

- A parent-teacher conference isn't held just to give out information about the child's school performance. It's also about listening to the parents. Oftentimes, next to the parents, you are the adult who knows their child the best.

- Don't hesitate to contact parents. Most parents are sincerely interested in how their child is doing in your class.

- If you suspect that a parent is doing a child's work for him, tactfully address the situation without making any accusations. Emphasize the fact that the child needs to be able to do his best work in class, too.

CHAPTER 18

Preparing for a Substitute Teacher

Few jobs are harder than being a substitute teacher assigned to a junior high or middle school classroom. Granted, this age group can be tough for even the regular teacher, but working with the same kids everyday enables a teacher to establish a discipline plan, a seating chart, and a working knowledge of what to expect. In addition, the regular teacher has leverage. When problems occur, parents can be called, and discipline threats can be acted upon.

For substitutes, there is no tomorrow, because most of the time they are in your classroom for only one day. Therefore, all situations must be resolved that day. Students know that. When students see a substitute teacher entering your classroom, they think, "What can they do to me? They are not going to be here tomorrow and besides, they don't even know for sure who I am. Yes, this is going to be fun." Often at the end of a day, substitute teachers are sure that the rock music classic "Born to Be Wild" was written about the students they faced that day.

Upon your return to the classroom, invariably a note is waiting for you from the substitute detailing a day of horror with the names of the star players highlighted. Usually you will find that although your replacement attempted to march through the lesson plans you left, little real education occurred. Supplies may be missing from your desk, and the classroom may look like an unfriendly army occupied it. Admittedly, this description resembles a worst-case scenario, and there are some effective substitute teachers who do an excellent job. However, it is likely that whenever you are gone, there will be problems unless you have made adjustments. This chapter explains what you need to do to prevent any major mishaps when you are not in class.

Providing Class Information

When a substitute teacher is in the classroom, students act out because they feel anonymous, believing that they can get away with stuff because the substitute teacher doesn't know their identities. Leaving an updated seating chart helps prevent this problem. If the substitute uses that to call on students by name, it becomes harder for students to get away with being in the wrong seat.

Staff members in adjacent rooms can help sub teachers. Early in the year, arrange with staff in nearby classrooms to introduce themselves to substitute teachers and offer their help. These staff can assist if there is a fire drill, bomb scare, or other building event that a sub might not know about. Occasionally a regular staff person may intercede on the substitute's behalf when there is an acute problem in the classroom. Leave the names and room numbers of these staff members in your instructions to the substitute teacher.

You should also supply the substitute with a brief description of your classroom policies. Be sure to indicate any items in the classroom that you do not want students to use. Note whether there are special instructions for certain equipment. For example, students often want to use computers when there is a substitute teacher. If you have a policy on Internet use, computer games, or e-mail, spell it out. Otherwise, students will create a policy for you.

Substitutes need to know how you deal with the use of room supplies. If you loan pencils, pens, and rulers or give out paper, rubber bands, and paper clips, indicate the procedure you use for this. Many a teacher has returned to her class to discover that her desk or room has been depleted of supplies.

Hall passes are another item that needs to be clarified. Students will immediately say that you have an "open door policy." All you need to do to leave the classroom is to ask, they'll tell the substitute, and permission is always granted. If you have a more restrictive plan, the substitute needs to know about it.

Substitute teachers welcome any ideas that will help them maintain classroom order. Including a brief description of the discipline system you use in your instructions to the substitute may be helpful. Giving the substitute some information about how you write names of misbehaving students on the board and then keep the miscreants a few minutes after class may make the substitute's day in your class more successful. If the substitute begins to control behavior using a system the students know and understand, they may behave better.

Assuming that the students will not see your instructions to the substitute, go ahead and leave them names of very cooperative students as well as those who might cause trouble. The cooperative ones will be able to tell the substitute how things ought to be, and the troublemakers are a good reference point if things start to go bad.

You don't need to write all of this information every time you are absent. If you prepare it at the beginning of the year, you can save it and have a copy printed each time you are gone. This chapter shows the instructions I used to give to my substitutes to give you an idea of what to include.

Instructions for Substitute Teachers

If you need help or information, your neighbors (John Heuker in room 102 and Aaron Whipple in room 106) will help you out. Look to them especially if you have a fire drill, a bomb scare, or a tornado drill.

Classes

Hours 1, 2, 3, and 5 are regular language arts classes.

Hour 4 is a low-level language arts class, and Tim O'Malley, a special education teacher, helps with this class. This class can be disruptive.

During the VIP hour Advisory class (Tuesday and Thursday only), students may study, or they may talk quietly. They are not allowed to play video or card games. Computers are only to be used for school projects.

Classroom Policies

Hall passes: Although I grant most requests, it is up to you. However, I don't let students interrupt my teaching to get a pass signed.

Classroom supplies: I allow students to take blank sheets of computer paper. But if they need a pencil, I ask that they leave something of value as collateral (wallets, keys, ID cards, money) so that they'll have a reason to return the pencil. I don't loan pens.

Computer use: Students may use computers only to do school assignments. During the VIP hour, they may use them to do work for other classes as well as language arts.

Behavior problems: Typically for minor disruptions, I write the students' names on the board and keep those named for about two minutes after class.

They should be in their correct seat. I'll try to have an updated seating chart on my desk with the lesson plans.

If you need detention slips, they are in the right-hand drawer of the desk, along with discipline referrals.

Please leave the names of disruptive students in your note to me along with a brief summary of what the problem was.

You can count on these students for help:

Hour 1: Britta Stifler, Katelyn Videto

Hour 2: Brittany Hunter, Lisa Wohlford

Hour 3: Hannah Figliomeni, Lucas Johnson

VIP: Kara Comstock, Caitlyn Bannister

Hour 4: Dawn Mongar, Jay Elliott

Hour 5: Scott Lumsden, Rachel Lepine

Leaving Lesson Plans

Sometimes you may know who your substitute will be or you can request a specific person. If your substitute is skilled at teaching your subject and is known to be effective at class management, you can dare to leave plans that will enable your replacement to actually teach a lesson so that your students will make some progress. More likely though, the substitute will have his hands full just trying to keep order.

Priority number one is supplying a lesson that will keep students occupied without being busywork. Students usually see busywork for what it is, and they don't take it seriously. Develop a plan that involves them doing work that is like what they would be doing if you were there. Reading assignments are excellent. Having them read and then respond in writing to what they have read works well. Try to make the assignment long enough so that most students won't finish during the class period. You can then have them complete the work when you're back. A writing project also can work well if students have a clear idea of what they are supposed to do. Videos or DVDs are good options, especially if they relate to the curriculum you are currently teaching.

Basic Lesson Plan

This plan is to be used only if there is no lesson plan on the teacher's desk in B-104 (Dave Foley's desk).

In the book *Adventures for Readers* (a kayaker is on the cover), have students read "The No-Talent Kid" on page 2 and answer the Seeking Meaning questions on page 11. These questions must be answered in complete sentences. The students also must restate the question as part of their answers. The answers should be thorough. If you are teaching for a second day and have received no plans, then discuss the story and the questions.

> TIP Giving kids free time or having them work in groups can be disastrous unless your substitute is a pro at classroom management. A day that you are absent is not the time to have unstructured class activities.

If you want work turned in, leave specific instructions about where and how this is to be done. Otherwise, when you inquire about missing work upon your return, you will hear laments such as, "She didn't tell us we had to turn it in," or "He said we could finish it later," or "I did turn it in. I put it right on your desk." If you know ahead of time that you are going to be absent, you can tell your students exactly what they will be doing and give them specifics for turning in the work.

Most of the times that teachers are absent, they will somehow get lesson plans into their room. They may be coughing, feeling dizzy, sweating bullets, and seemingly experiencing the final stages of the plague, yet they will still be scribbling out instructions for their replacement. In the unlikely event that you are so indisposed that leaving a substitute plan is impossible, you can fall back on your all-purpose generic lesson.

This lesson is self-explanatory, can be delivered by anyone, and keeps students earnestly working for two days. Write this plan during the first week of school and place it in a folder that will be given to the substitute if it becomes apparent that there is no other plan left by you. The following is my plan, which has been used only once or twice in 30 years.

In my school's office, each teacher had a folder that was given to substitutes when they checked into the building. It included the teacher's seating chart, daily schedule, basic discipline plan, and detention and discipline write-up forms. In addition, there was the generic class lesson with instructions attached to it, telling the substitute not to use it unless there was no lesson plan on the teacher's desk.

Summary

The difficulty of trying to prepare lesson plans for your absence and then having to deal with the aftermath of what happened in your classroom while you were gone can be a powerful incentive never to be absent. When you do have to miss a day of school, use the ideas in this chapter to make the best of it:

- At the beginning of the year, prepare an information sheet for substitutes that describes your classroom polices and lists the names of helpful teachers and students.

- Ideally, you want to leave a lesson plan for the substitute that will keep the students occupied and will be related to what you are currently teaching in class.

INDEX

About the Author

Dave Foley taught English and social studies at junior high and middle schools in Cadillac, Michigan, for 29 years. Like all teachers, he faced the daily behavioral challenges from his students. Then, after watching his student teachers struggle to keep the classroom under control, Foley realized these teaching novices needed help. To give these teachers solutions to student behavior problems and procedures for running a classroom without chaos, Foley began drafting this book. Methodically, Foley began to study the daily minor annoyances and the occasional serious disturbances that occurred in classrooms. He then noted, in detail, teacher responses that solved the problem.

As a result of his success in the classroom, the school administration asked Foley to present workshops during new teacher orientation dealing with student behavior and classroom management. Central Michigan University brought Foley in to make a presentation to its student teachers on classroom management and strategies for dealing with student behavior problems.

In 2002, teachers in the Cadillac, Michigan, School District named Foley the "Outstanding Person in Education."

As head varsity coach for cross-country for 27 years and junior high and varsity track coach for 9 years, Foley has countless hours of close contact with adolescents in non-academic settings. Foley also worked as a camp counselor for 9 years prior to becoming a teacher. His years at camp enabled him to deal effectively with student behavior problems as a teacher. In recent years, Foley has returned to the camp setting, where he now works with three camps presenting workshops to camp staff designed to help them deal effectively with camper behavior problems.

Foley holds a Master's Degree in Guidance and Counseling at Michigan State University. He is known for his engaging and entertaining speaking style in the classroom and before groups.